The Aerial Circus Training and Safety Manual

A Guide for Teachers and Students

By

Carrie Heller, M.S.W.

Photos by Richard Lubrant

National Writers Press

Copyright © 2004 Aerial Circus Training and Safety Manual; A Guide for Teachers and Students by Carrie Heller

All rights reserved, which includes the right to reproduce this book or portions thereof in any form whatsoever except as provided by the U.S. Copyright Law. For information contact: National Writers Press, 17011 Lincoln Avenue, #421, Parker, Colorado 80134.

Published in the United States of America by Circus Arts Institute

In Conjunction With:
National Writers Press
17011 Lincoln Avenue, #421
Parker, Colorado 80134 USA

Cover Design by
NZ Graphics, www.nzgraphics.com
Lakewood, Colorado USA
Special Thanks to Nick Zelinger

Photographs by Richard Lubrant
Photos in Single Point Trapeze Section by Don Carson

LIBRARY OF CONGRESS CATALOGING-IN-PUBLICATION DATA

Aerial Circus Safety and Training Manual/ by Carrie Heller
International Standard Book Number (ISBN 10): 0-88100-136-8
International Standard Book Number (ISBN 13): 978-0-88100-136-5

1. Performing Arts   2. Reference   3. Education & Teaching   1. Title
                                                              2005906914

     4   5   6   7   8   9   10

Foreword

This year I was fortunate enough to come into possession of Archange Tuccaro's *Trois Dialogues de l'exercise de sauter et de voltiger en l'air* [Paris, 1599], the first book ever written and published exclusively on the subject of aerobatics. Last year I obtained Alberto Zucca's *Acrobatica e athletica* [Milano, 1902], another rare, and valuable item to grace my circus library. Some time ago I got hold of Georges Strehly's *L'Acrobatie et les acrobates* [Paris, n.d. (1903), reprinted 1977]. Zucca mentions Tuccaro, and Strehly mentions both Tuccaro and Zucca. So it goes. In *Aerial Circus Safety and Training Manual*, Carrie Heller is kind enough to mention my *Circus Techniques* [1976]. It seems as if she has, more-or-less, taken my "Rigging Equilibristics" chapter, and expanded it fifteen-fold, adding numerous features and improvements entirely her own.

You have before you a safety manual with lifesaving tips on how to spot. Here is a "how-to" primer covering all the basic moves and terminology. Here are photographic studies of advanced aerialists at work. If you teach aerial work; if you perform, or exercise, on aerial circus rigging; if you are an aficionado, or historian, of such activities: this book is for you.

Whoever first said that a little knowledge is a dangerous thing might very well have been thinking of trapeze and other aerial work. Far too many "barmaids" performing at inns and taverns made notices in the 19th century British obituary columns simply because they were insufficiently prepared to emulate the work of such aerials stars as the American-born Leona Dare or Miss Lala, immortalized on canvas oil by Edgar Degas, hanging by her teeth at Cirque Fernando in 1879. Risk, risk-taking and calculating risk are all part of life. Carrie Heller completely instructs us in trapeze and other equipment, while she wisely exhorts us to think safety (first, last and always).

Hovey Burgess
Master Teacher of Circus and author of *Circus Techniques*
New York University

DISCLAIMER: In doing any aerial trick there is a real chance of injury no matter how "safe" or experienced you are and no matter who is spotting or teaching you. The author, or anyone else whose advice was used in writing this manual, will not be responsible for any injury or misunderstanding resulting from the practice or performance of any feats described in this work-which includes every single page and movement seen in this manual. Purchase or use of this document constitutes agreement of this effect. Furthermore, the author does not use or discuss safety lines in this document. The author advises consulting a professional rigger when it comes to using any safety lines or hanging equipment.

Preface

This manual has come about over several decades of instructing many individuals to teach the aerial arts. I first learned trapeze, web, tightwire and rings when I was a child at Camp Keystone in Florida...where students from the FSU Flying High Circus had a rig set up for teaching. I enjoyed it so much I began teaching in Atlanta after receiving a Masters Degree in Social Work. I then started noticing all of the self-esteem benefits in addition to the fun everyone was having while playing on the equipment. In time I started a summer day camp so that any child could come and experience the thrill of learning the arts of the circus. With the camp serving over 1000 children on our 10th anniversary, I began teaching more and more individuals how to spot aerials using this manual. Over time many of the teachers I was working with requested that I photograph the manual and, as a result, this book has come to be.

This is in no way shape or form a complete list of every trick available to the circus world. That would be impossible as each artist is probably making up a new trick with each new workout. This is simply a gathering of the tricks I have learned and made up, as well as tricks and information that others have shared with me that I have compiled over the years.

The main focus of the book is on the Trapeze, Spanish Web, and Rings as this has been my specialty over the years. I have included a sampling of other pieces of equipment as examples of what else can be learned.

My thanks to my parents, Dr. E. Maurice & Barbara Heller and my brother Andy for their encouragement, inspiration, support and love.

My thanks to Connie Amos who provided me the space at Camp Keystone in Odessa, Florida to learn the aerial arts as a child; to my original teachers Beth McEvoy Brinson, students of the FSU Flying High Circus, and the other patient and talented teachers who I crossed paths with over the years.

My thanks to MagicSteve Ringel, Deva Joy Gouss, Allen Rosenthal, Allison and Jeffree Gars for their ongoing and tireless support and to Michael Jamison for his guidance in the martial arts.

My thanks to those who contributed directly to this manual: Many circus folk were good enough to read over the text, edit, add and/or model for the project. Thank you to Hovey Burgess for his guidance, editing and encouragement throughout this project. My deepest thanks to all of the students and teachers of my Circus Arts program and summer camp in Atlanta, Georgia. Thanks specifically goes out to those photographed in this manual: Ellen Rosenthal, Morgaine Rosenthal, Feliza Rosenthal, Deborah Hurley, Shad Sterling, Sara Gregory, Hilary Huff-Riall, Joanna Glasser, Lauren Baker, Willow Hagemeier Goldstein, Eli Zandman, Chantal Igherighe, Zack Riedford, and Teresa Kochis. To Cindy Alana Brannon and Lauren Baker for modeling and providing descriptions of their tricks for this book. Thank you to the folks from Camp Winnarainbow in California and teachers Anne Seward, Saharah Moon Chapotin, Allison Allbee, and Teresa Dinaburg for their feedback and contributions to this book. Thank you to Susan Murphy for the Single Point Trapeze Section, Don Carson and Steve Pomberg for additional photos, as well as Carl, Jake, Mary, and Annette Conover from Custom Built Equipment for their feedback and contributions to this book.

Thank you to Kevin and Erin Maile O'Keefe for their support and encouragement. I would also like to recognize AYCO-the American Youth Circus Organization for all its work toward bringing circus to our youth. AYCO is a community-based nonprofit organization that promotes the participation of youth in circus arts. AYCO relies on modest membership fees, grants, and the generosity of thousands of volunteer hours to support its efforts. Please join us in our conversation about youth circus, social circus, safety and standards, and more by becoming an AYCO community member. Find us at www.americanyouthcirucs.org/member.htm to register. AYCO has produced two very successful festivals to date with more on the way. We are all grateful to Kevin and Erin for the time and energy they have dedicated to this project.

Thank you to Richard Lubrant for his patience, humor and supreme talent as a photographer.

Special thanks to Karen Horvat for spending countless hours editing this book for me as well as for being one of my most photographed models. Special thanks to Nancy Neyhart for editing as well as to Karen Horvat for both editing and for being one of my most photographed models. Many thanks to Mary Ann Hart for doing several test runs over the years of this manual, for being one of my most photographed models and for her contributions to the editing process.

Many thanks to Serenity Smith Forchion and Elsie Smith for their contributions on proper technique and injury prevention, for modeling and providing descriptions of their tricks for this book, and for their ongoing contributions and feedback to all editions of this manual.

I would like to recognize Dr. Reg Bolton who pioneered the concept of New Circus authoring the seminal book *Circus In a Suitcase*. Reg then went on to complete his PhD in Social Circus. Reg was not only a great personality but an inspiration to the circus community. He will be greatly missed.

This book is in honor and in memory of my Father, Dr. E. Maurice Heller. My father's credentials made him a Cardiologist, while those who knew him had the privilege of knowing a true healer. I thank my father for teaching me about kindness as well as service to the community. It was from my father that I learned about Mastery of one's calling in life, as well as the most important lesson of all; that we must ALWAYS work towards peace.

With Peace and Flight,
Carrie Heller
Carrie@CircusArtsInstitute.com
www.circusartsinstitute.com

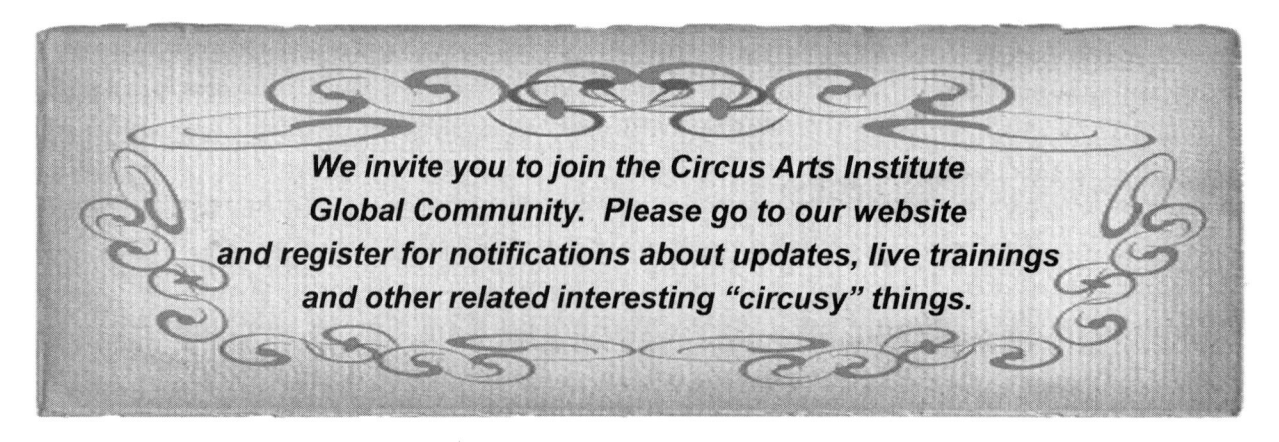

We invite you to join the Circus Arts Institute Global Community. Please go to our website and register for notifications about updates, live trainings and other related interesting "circusy" things.

TABLE OF CONTENTS

Foundation of A Circus Arts Program 5

How To Use This Manual 7

Check Your Rig & Equipment! 10

Safety and Spotting 12

Warm Ups & Cool Downs 18
    General 19
    Chi Kung 20
    Sample Stretches and Yoga Warmups 24

Trapeze 40
    Equipment 41
    Instructor Notes 43
    Tricks & Combinations 49
    Samples: Advanced Trapeze 163
    Double Trapeze 167
    Single Point Trapeze (aka Dance Trapeze) 176

Spanish Web 180
    Equipment 181
    Instructor Notes 182

Rings 264
    Equipment 265
    Instructor Notes 266
    Tricks 267

Tissu Samples 301

Lyra Samples 309

Tightwire Samples 315

Trick Levels 321

Index of Tricks 329

FOUNDATIONS OF A CIRCUS ARTS PROGRAM

As an aerialist and a Licensed Clinical Social Worker, I have some very specific goals in mind when teaching the arts of the circus. I want each student to walk out of each class having accomplished something. I wish for each student to have fun and to grow as an individual as a result of his or her experience in Circus Arts. The foundation and philosophy of my program are outlined in the goals below:

1. Increase self-confidence and self-respect.
2. Help students to move through their fears. When someone moves through a fear of doing a cradle on the trapeze or a hand balancing trick with a partner, this experience is transferred to their everyday life.
3. Tap into the body/mind connection.
4. Love of self and of one's own body.
5. All tricks are taught at each student's individual pace. As often as possible, students are grouped into classes by age and/or rate of physical learning.
6. Circus Arts is a NONCOMPETITIVE activity. Although there are Beginner, Intermediate and Advanced tricks and these levels of progress can be pointed out, it is practiced in a noncompetitive way. Every step a student takes toward learning a new skill or trick is acknowledged, and the slightest movement toward a goal is congratulated.
7. We help students to take risks physically and emotionally (for example, try a trick that they previously thought they could not do) in a safe environment.
8. Body balancing is a core part of my program. Students learn every skill and trick on both sides of the body. When performing, students usually prefer to perform tricks on the side they are most adept at; however, it is imperative that students are taught to rehearse on both sides of the body to keep the body balanced. Most tricks in this manual are photographed on one side, although in a few instances I show both sides.
9. BREATHING is stressed. Often students hold their breath while doing a trick. Remember to inhale before a trick and exhale as you go into a trick. Breathe while you are in a trick and exhale as you exert energy to come out of a trick. It's OK to breathe so you can actually be heard breathing.
10. In "Aerial Circus" or "Aerial Dance," one of the basic principles of spinning is the following: As the body opens, the movement slows down. As the body closes, the movement speeds up. Knowing this principle will allow you to help control your rotation and/or spin on the trapeze, rings and the web.
11. Circus Arts teaches balance, timing, flexibility, strength building, acrobatics, creative movement, and tricks on the equipment. This is all done in a FUN and safe environment.
12. SAFETY is *always stressed.*

HOW TO USE THIS MANUAL

The tricks in this manual are the most common tricks taught in Circus class. The tricks are presented in progression from beginning to more advanced, and in some cases demonstrate prerequisite movements. When learning trapeze, web, or rings, I advise each student to first complete the first lesson, as outlined in this manual, before moving on to other tricks.

The order presented in this manual is designed to help create a progression of increased strength, flexibility, balance, and self-confidence while playing on circus equipment.

Your choice of which tricks to do beyond the first lesson will vary from student to student. As is the case with all physical movements, certain individuals will have particular preferences regarding which moves they will choose to do or to not do. This is often based on personal preference and abilities.

AUTHOR'S NOTE:

I advise you NOT to try any of these tricks without first taking classes or a workshop with an experienced Aerial instructor. This manual is designed for instructors, performers, choreographers, and students who are studying in Aerial Circus. Most of the tricks photographed in this manual are purposely photographed with spotters. The intention of this manual is to teach the aerial tricks to the student AND to teach the teacher and spotter options for spotting in a safe manner. Once you become proficient at a trick enough to become, for example, a performer, it is no longer necessary to have a spotter. Similarly, once you master the fundamentals and proper technique, you can begin to improvise and choreograph some of your own moves as is seen by some of those photographed in this manual. Sometimes it is easy to choreograph a spotter into an aerial piece to be performed, sometimes it is not. Therefore, there are examples throughout this manual of Advanced Aerialists demonstrating tricks without spotters. However, it is most important to always be safe and, when in doubt, make sure you have a spotter even if you are an experienced performer.

Finally, in some cases, spotters in this manual are positioned a step or two away from the student for the photographic needs of this manual. The position and how to spot is indicated by the photo; however, please note that it is necessary to be CLOSE enough to your student so that you can properly spot and break their fall if necessary, on all occasions. Consequently, when viewing the position of the spotters, be advised that it will be necessary (in most cases) for you to take a step or two CLOSER to your student on the equipment so that you can spot them with greater ease. As a spotter you must have your hands on the student whenever they are doing a new trick.

About the tricks in this manual:

Many of the tricks in this manual are considered standard circus tricks. Some are done in the standard circus way, while others, you will notice, are more in line with what I call "Aerial Dance." For example: in standard circus, feet are routinely flexed when doing a cradle. In Aerial Dance, the toes are sometimes pointed when doing a cradle. Similarly, when climbing the Spanish Web it is recommended that you flex the foot to get a better grip, however some prefer to "sickle" the foot. Technically, it is harder to climb with sickled feet but some do prefer to do it this way. The important thing is to be aware of the choices and differences and the implications of each choice you make.

Some tricks may be identified by more than one name. During my travels and the travels of some of my students and other teachers and performers who have edited this book, it has come to my attention that a trick that we call, for example; Mermaid is called a Dragon Catcher in California, or a Hip Hang, is called a Single Knee Lay Back in one circus school, and an Amazon or a Gazelle by yet another teacher in another circus school. Whenever it has come to my attention, I have provided every name that I have heard beside each trick. This can be rather confusing at times; however, there ARE many people teaching circus around the world and new tricks are created every day and old tricks are sometimes taught under different names by different teachers. Students have come through my studio over the years from the all over the United States as well as from parts of Canada, Australia and Europe; so I have seen first hand that the exact same trick can be called 5 different names!

Many of the tricks in this manual are made up, either by me or one of my students. In such cases we have also made up the names of such tricks. And finally, a few tricks are named after those individuals that I learned the trick from. For example, The Serenity Swing is a trick I learned from Serenity Smith Forchion when I was visiting San Francisco many years ago. Honestly I don't know if Serenity made it up or someone else taught her the trick, I only know that I think of her whenever I teach it to someone else, and therefore I decided to name the trick after her. Besides I think "The Serenity Swing" is a good name for that particular trick! (See web section). Another example of this is the "Freedman Flag" which is named after one of my students named Allen Freedman. Allen made this trick up one day in class and one of my students named it after him. Similarly, Cindy Alana, one of my most gifted aerial students turned performer, created her own unique combination on the Spanish Web. You will see this in the Web section entitled "Cindy Alana's Combination."

Have fun and be safe!!

CHECK YOUR RIG & EQUIPMENT!

A. Professional Rig Check

It is beyond the scope of this manual to describe in detail all the possible rigs. Below are some general recommendations:

-Rigging is to be checked at least once a year by a professional, insured rigger. At this time there are no published standards for circus rigging; therefore, it is best to get a recommendation from another aerialist for a rigger who is familiar with aerial.

-Make sure you check references.

-If you ever have a question that is beyond your expertise, find someone who can answer it. This may include consulting with your professional rigger, a welder, an experienced aerialist or an engineer.

-It is good for students who are pursuing more serious aerial studies to have a basic knowledge of the rig. The more serious the student, the more s/he must know about a rig. Even if they do no rigging as a part of your program, this is part of learning to be an aerialist, especially if the student is interested in setting up his or her own equipment. Meet any of their questions about the rigging with serious respect and intelligent answers. If your program does not allow for you to teach them these basics, or if you do not feel qualified to do so, inform the serious aerial student about the importance of safety and that they must learn about their rig if they are to have one.

B. Equipment Check

-It is important to know the rig you are using and/or teaching on.

-As an Aerial Circus teacher or performer you are responsible for inspecting your equipment on a regular basis. Teach your assistants to do the same.

-Schedule your inspection at a time when things are quiet and you are free from distractions.

-Teach every person you work with to be very focused and respectful and out of harm's way when anyone is up on the rig for an equipment change. Make sure that no one is under the rig when you lower equipment. Always call out before you lower the equipment or anything from the top of the rig. Never drop any portion of your rigging. It can cause damage to the rigging and injuries to your co-workers. Equipment should be lowered by rope or by hand to the floor. Develop a call and response with your co-workers so you know that they heard you and that they are aware something is coming down.

-Whatever rope and attachments you use, it is imperative that load capacities of the beams and ceiling from which you are hanging be checked. Make sure to get quoted capacity when in 'swing' not just static. A good rule of thumb is that the rigging must be able to withstand a force of 5 times your body weight if static, and 10 times your body weight if a dynamic (moving) load is applied. Then give yourself a safety margin of twice that total. Example: a 150 lb. person on Rings doing a dynamic act would need all the parts of his equipment to be able to withstand a minimum of 3000 lbs. For those in northern climates, be aware how a snow load will affect ceiling dynamics.

-ALWAYS double check any rigging changes that are made. Even the best people in the world can make a mistake.

-Keep a log of regular inspections of equipment.

SAFETY & SPOTTING

A. Before You Begin

1. Explain this at the students' first class:

Circus Arts is a really fun place to be. It is also unlike any other activity you have ever done. Therefore there are some special things you need to know before we start class:

   a. Instructor/spotter must ALWAYS be present before going on any equipment or before doing any acrobatics. This means the instructor/spotter must be RIGHT THERE beside your body and sometimes there must be more than one spotter present.
   b. Use a mat or padded floor when doing aerial equipment or acrobatics.
   c. It is important to always warm up and stretch before doing any tricks and cool down and stretch afterward. It's always a good idea to ask the students if they know why this is important. If no one knows (which is very unlikely) tell them this helps prevent injury.
   d. **PAST OR PRESENT MEDICAL PROBLEMS, INJURIES OR TRAUMA-** Inquire if anyone has any physical problems before starting your first class. If a student is under 18, ask parents or have this question on an application form that parents fill out. Back troubles, recent wrist, ankle injuries, and abdominal surgeries are all things to know about that may affect a student's ability to do certain tricks. If a student informs you of a problem on that day, consult with your lead instructor as to what the student may or may not be able to do that particular day.
   e. It is never OK to joke about accidents or falling. Occasionally someone will joke about falling when someone is performing or changing rigging. This is not OK. It is very important for all persons who choose to be around the aerial arts to be supportive and of a positive mindset.

   NOTE to all teachers: If you run a Circus School, Circus Camp or are doing any sort of instruction, I HIGHLY RECOMMEND having insurance and I suggest you consult with a lawyer about Liability Releases and Emergency Procedures.

B. Spotting

1. Levels of Ability

Be aware of different levels of physical abilities of the students; for example, flexibility, strength, physical confidence, previous physical activity with their bodies, as well as kinesthetic awareness of their bodies. This can usually be determined by observing someone or by the information that they volunteer to you. However, if you feel like you need more information, feel free to inquire. The kinetic memory is very powerful and you will find it is a big part of learning aerial arts. It helps with any student to ask if they did anything similar in the past, like the jungle gym bars at school. It is amazing to see how this comes back. Even after 30 years, some people will just do what they did as a kid automatically and without thinking about it.

Always stress that strength varies from day to day. Physical abilities are based on many things such as emotional states, diet, sleep, etc. Give praise and respect to students for their ability to asses their own energy levels. Tell them, if they do not feel strong enough or comfortable doing a trick, then don't do it. Really watch for this during performances. One thing you may see with children in a summer program is a student who has grown a lot over the past year. Their body has changed and they may not be able to do the same things that they did the previous summer.

2. Positioning

Tricks in this manual are almost always demonstrated with a spotter. There are many ways to spot someone on a piece of equipment. You must spot in the way that you are most comfortable and the way in which your teacher has advised you to spot. Some basic principles I always focus on when teaching others to spot include but are not limited to:

   a. Position yourself in such a way that you would be capable of 'breaking a fall' if a student were to fall off (see #8), or so that your hand is in a position to interrupt, for example, a leg from flying upward and propelling the body into the air (see Trapeze T03). You will see a wide variety of positions and ways to spot demonstrated in this manual. Choose what works best for you as you integrate the principles I have outlined in this manual.

   b. In positioning yourself, keep in mind which part of the student's body will fall to the ground first. For example, in a cradle on the bar, a student's tummy is closest to the ground. It is therefore advisable to place your hand, as a spotter, directly under the tummy when spotting a cradle while at the same time looking to see if the student's hands and ankles are securely attached. If not, then it is important to shift your hands to the place where the student's contact is slipping to provide assistance. If someone falls, spot the most vulnerable part. Be concerned about the head and neck and support that more than if the feet hit the ground.

   c. Be focused, alert and ready at all times. It is impossible to completely prepare for a student falling. You must do your best to be extremely alert and tuned in to all points where student makes contact with the equipment.

   d. Be aware (to the best of your ability) of the level of strength and fitness of each student you are working with. This will help you to gauge when the student might be getting a little tired.

   e. When in doubt… OVERSPOT. If you feel like you need another spotter to spot a certain trick, do not let the student do the trick until another spotter is available.

3. Demonstrate all Tricks

Teacher demonstrates or has a more advanced student demonstrate new tricks. Demonstration allows the observing student to build a mental picture of the correct form of all tricks and accelerates the learning process. The photos in this manual are all UNDER SPOTTED so you can see the tricks. Be sure to have hands on and imagine actually catching someone falling.

4. Special Needs Students

Often students with particular needs come to Circus class. For example, a student who has trouble focusing. Most of the time you will know about this and, when appropriate, please advise all of the instructors/spotters of a particular student's needs. However, parents do not always inform us of these issues unless it comes up. If you have any concerns or questions about a particular student, feel free to ask. The goal here is to simply teach the Circus skills as well as to keep the philosophy in mind at all times. This always includes safety and personal growth, both physical and emotional, in the healthiest manner possible.

5. Communication with Students

Check in periodically with students while they are on the equipment. Circus is a lot more tiring than most activities. Ask someone "how's your arm strength doing?" Many students will be able to say "I'm tired, I need to come down." However, others will not be able to tell you this, so you (Instructor/spotter) must use your intuition. If your intuition says the student is done for now, then ask them to come down and take a rest. On the other hand, if a student tells you they are tired, always have them come down. It is important to take their word for it because, for whatever reason, they feel they are done for the moment. They simply might be tired on this particular day more so than on another occasion.

Whenever you are spotting a student, it is important to maintain contact with him or her as much as possible, both physically and verbally. Verbally you are giving them the necessary directions for each movement plus consistent positive reinforcement. Physically you are guiding them through the movement and spotting them. Many people are afraid of heights. If they have not told you so, and you suspect it, go EXTRA SLOW—BABY STEPS. Everyone must go at their own pace, even if it appears exceptionally slow to you.

If you are the spotter of a particular piece of equipment, you are in charge. The lead instructor is available to help with decisions; however, you are in charge while you are spotting. It is important to take control of a situation.

6. Give Positive Feedback

Always give positive feedback!!! Give positive reinforcement for every single small step a student takes -- every inch up the web, etc... For example, encourage your students that even climbing the web is a big accomplishment.

Consistently motivate students to reach their potential and learn new tricks at their own pace. Allow students to have their fear, then help them move through it no matter how long or how many Circus classes it takes.

7. Breaking a Fall versus Catching a Student

Often the spotter will 'break' a student's fall rather than actually catching a student in his or her arms. With smaller children it is often easy to actually catch them if they miss a trick. If a student is much larger it might not be possible to fully catch him or her. Instead, your goal is to break their fall as you spot them; head and neck are most important. The student may still end up on the mat, but your intervention will reduce the impact of the fall dramatically.

8. Boo Boo's or Falls

If a student ever injures himself or herself, whether it is a small cut or literally falling off the equipment and bruising, notify the lead instructor immediately. Do not get over excited if an injury occurs . Students can easily pick up on your reactions and it could cause things to get out of hand. First Aid courses are a good foundation for all teachers just as having an emergency procedure in place is important as well.

If a student ever falls or slips out of a trick or off a piece of equipment, it is important to ask the student to go back up and repeat the movement the way it was taught to them. It is important that a student's last memory of doing that particular movement is a positive body memory rather than an incomplete or negative one. The only exception is if a student is too tired (in which case you encourage them to do it before the class period is over) or if a part of their body is sore or has been injured in the fall (in which case you encourage them to repeat the movement or "trick" the next class time whenever possible).

C. Body Balancing

All tricks are done in balance with the whole body. For example: on the trapeze, side lay backs are done on both sides; splits are done with one leg forward then other leg forward; and ¼ (T16) or ½ (T37) Angels are learned on both sides. On the web, all handwork and footwork is learned using both the right and left hands and feet. Also, a body wrap, like the Diaper Wrap (W19), is learned with the right and then the left (or visa versa) leg leading. The goal is to keep the body balanced so that we are teaching individuals to use both sides of their bodies equally. Furthermore, if the body is not balanced, it can lead to increased risk of injury. Please explain this to all students as you are instructing them.

D. Performing

The excitement of a performance brings with it more adrenaline and distraction than class time. It is important to prepare your students for this. Rehearsal is the best way to prepare for the performance. A key goal is for each student to know his or her routine/trick(s) or moves well enough so that it is "in" his/her body.

Help prepare the students to stay focused with basic breathing exercises and visualizations.

Teach your class to become an attentive audience. Teach them to be respectful and supportive of the person who is performing. Encourage them to applaud for each other; they know more than anyone how difficult these tricks are. Know exactly what each student is going to perform and do not let him or her try any new or unrehearsed tricks. There is a great tendency toward overconfidence during performing, just as there is a tendency toward nervousness. Both of these tendencies must be watched out for as they can become a safety issue if not attended to.

As a teacher it is important for you to do a safety check and rigging rehearsal to insure that you are as calm and focused as possible during a performance.

E. Safety

1. Do not put lotion or moisturizers on hands before going on equipment. It can make you slip and it can damage the equipment and create a safety hazard that could be avoided.
2. If you have a cut, even a minor one, always put on a bandage before going on equipment.
3. Remember to always do endurance and strength tests before students progress on the Spanish web to high loop activities (detailed in Spanish Web section), or similarly to rope work on the trapeze.
4. Students must review the basics if they have not been on the equipment for a significant period of time, no matter how advanced they were.
5. Focus on Breathing. There is a tendency to hold your breath while doing tricks. Make sure to breathe!
6. If you are shaking, or see a student shaking while on equipment, this means the muscles are tired. Ask them to come down off equipment and rest.
7. Ask students who are experimenting to go extra slow and inform you of what they are doing so that you may spot them correctly.
8. Be sure to drink enough water.
9. ALWAYS warm up your body and then stretch before a workout (minimum 10 minutes), and do more of an extensive cool down the more you work out. It is also recommended that you keep the body moving and warm in between your turns on the equipment.

10. Watch out for jewelry. Rule of thumb: if questionable, take it off. I ask all my students to remove all necklaces and chains, bracelets, and rings.
11. No chewing gum or candy.
12. Regarding the use of gymnastic chalk and rosin: If you choose to use either, be aware that rosin often is a bit stickier which is more preferable to prevent slipping down ropes, whether they be trapeze ropes or Web.

PLEASE NOTE: When teaching, I rarely use safety lines. All of my teaching trapezes and rings are about 5'2" off the ground. I instruct all of my teachers to spot from this position. When trapezes or rings are higher, I advise using safety lines. The use of safety lines is not a part of this book. There are demonstrations of how to beat up on a higher bar in addition to some sample tricks on additional apparatus. I have included these examples to demonstrate that there is a lot to do on higher equipment and other pieces of equipment not fully covered in this manual.

THERE IS NO SUCH THING AS BEING TOO CAREFUL.

NEVER BE AFRAID TO STOP WHAT IS GOING ON FOR SAFETY.

WARM UPS & COOL DOWNS

GENERAL

1. Always begin with an aerobic warm up by walking around room, jumping rope or the like to get the blood flowing to literally "warm the body." It is essential not to stretch the body before a warm up as the body is cold and this could cause injury!
2. I also like to include some basic Chi Kung (pronounced "chee-gong") exercises before stretching. Chi Kung is a unique and ancient Chinese healing tradition and fitness art that has been passed down from generation to generation for over three thousand years. It is known to enhance the immune system functioning through the body's 'chi' or 'vital force'. I recommend that all my students include some Chi Kung exercises in their warmup as it is a wonderful way of warming up the body "from the inside out." I especially recommend doing Chi Kung in between your time on the equipment. In other words, instead of standing still or sitting , it is best to keep the body warm and the energy flowing in between your time on the equipment. Stretching, yoga and Chi Kung are good for this. (Examples on following page).
3. A full body stretch is led by trained instructor. Be advised that for some it is better to NOT stretch certain parts of the body; like, for example the Shoulders. "Warm Up" shoulders rather than "stretch" already flexible shoulders. Please see "Shoulder Stretches" for more information on this.
4. All staff are asked to fully participate in warm up, stretch, and cool down. Also for staff safety be prepared (stretched) to demonstrate. You are role models for the students. If you see a student having difficulty or unable to do a stretch, take it upon yourself to go right up to them and assist.
5. End warm up with backbends since many of the circus tricks require flexibility in the back. All instructors must be trained to spot backbends. If you are unsure of proper backbend technique or how to spot a backbend, please consult with the lead instructor. Always do a backbend from laying down BEFORE allowing student to do one from standing. This allows for the back to have a proper gentle stretch.
6. I use a variety of techniques in my circus warm ups including basic stretches, yoga postures, Chi Kung exercises, and playful movements (i.e. leap like a frog). Asking students to come up with stretches to share with the class tends to make the class more fun for the participants.
7. Cool down and stretch after your workout.
8. Always maintain Proper Body Position: see Trapeze section with Elsie and Serenity.
9. Always stretch both sides of the body. Photos mostly show examples on one side.

CHI KUNG

(also spelled Qi Gong) pronounced 'chee-gong'. Chi Kung is a unique and ancient Chinese healing tradition and fitness art that has been passed down from generation to generation for over three thousand years.

I would like to thank my Chi Kung teacher, Michael Jamison for teaching me this unique and energizing form of movement.

In this section I am including only a sampling of Chi Kung exercises. There are many more to learn if you choose to do so:
Recommended Reading: *QIGONG- For Health and Vitality*
Author: Michael Tse
Published by St. Martin's Press, 175 Fifth Avenue, New York, N.Y. 10010

Warming up the Spine

Photos 1 & 2: Bouncing (which achieves similar results as *The Spinal Rock,* pictured on the next page) helps to move the cerebral spinal fluid inside your spine, which then nourishes and stimulates all the nerves in the body to help revitalize and/or "wake up" the system. You will notice we are also vibrating our lips which warms up the face and relaxes the jaw (and also ultimately makes you laugh).

Photo 3:
Similar to **Photos 1 & 2**, we are gently bouncing here, while placing the back side of our hands at the base of the spine to gently massage as we bounce up and down.

Spinal Rock AKA Tuck

Photo 1: Sit straight up and hug knees.

Photo 2: Begin to roll backwards.

Photo 3: Continue rolling backwards.

NOTE: Never roll further than top of shoulders as this puts strain on the neck.

Photo 4: Roll back up.

Waist

Above is a gentle stretch for the waist that is also a Chi Kung exercise.

Brain Balancing

Many Circus activities, most notably juggling, are wonderful brain balancing activities. Chi Kung offers many exercises to help balance the brain which has many benefits. There are several books written just on this subject. It is such an important part of learning and body awareness that I have included a little information on Brain Balancing here and an example in this photo.

1. When you learn everything on both sides, it will help in learning other things more quickly, not to mention all the other benefits of being ambidextrous. I stress throughout this manual learning all tricks on both sides of the body (Body Balancing), not only to help prevent overuse of one side of your body and thus hopefully lessen your chances of being injured, but also for Brain Balancing benefits.
2. Brain balancing exercises help to prepare the brain for better learning.
3. Many of the exercises are designed to help the brain integrate both the right and the left sides. This forces the brain to work more holistically, more as a whole. The idea is to have the whole brain working together. This is inspired by cross lateral movements.
4. Being ambidextrous will help you open up the brain on both sides and use more of your brainpower.

Photo: In this photo we are balancing on one foot, while shaking the foot in the air and the opposite hand at the same time. In this exercise we are not only warming up the leg and arm, but we are also engaging in a Brain Balancing activity. Remember to do it on the other side as well.

SAMPLE STRETCHES
Wrists & Forearms

Photo 1: Gently lean into hands.

Photo 2: With forearms facing up, use hand of other arm to gently press fingers down.

Isolate forearms by keeping elbows close to waist.

Photo 3: With forearm facing down and hand in a fist, use hand of other arm to gently press fist down.

Photos 1-5: Clasp hands together interlacing fingers and thumb. Gently roll wrists around in circles.

Foot & Ankle

Place your foot in a position where you can easily roll the ankle in a circle. Be sure to rotate your foot in both directions.

Hips & Legs

Photo(s) 1: One knee is bent and other leg straight behind. Place same hand next to knee while leaning into the hip of straight leg supported by same hand/arm. This is a wonderful stretch for the iliopsoas.

Photo(s) 2: Bend back leg up and hold with opposite hand stretching the quadriceps while continuing to support upper body with other arm.

Caution: Although this is one of my students' and my favorite stretches, please be advised that there are some stretching programs that do not teach this due to knee torque.

Photo 3: While supporting self on one knee, straighten other leg out in front. With straight back lean forward and support self with hands on the floor to stretch the hamstrings.

27

The Forward Bend AKA Pike

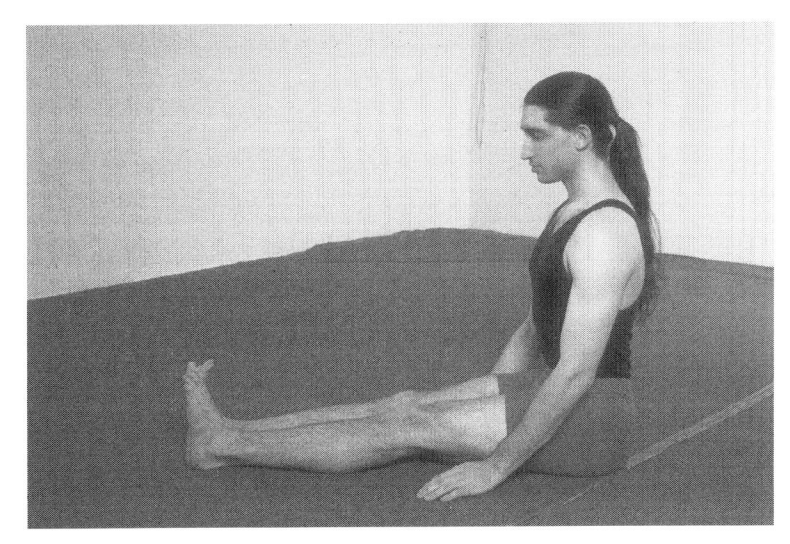

Photo 1: Sit up with legs straight out in front. Reach head toward ceiling while reaching sacrum toward ground.

Photo 2: Keeping back straight and head reaching away from sacrum, flex feet and begin to lean forward. Continue reaching sacrum toward floor.

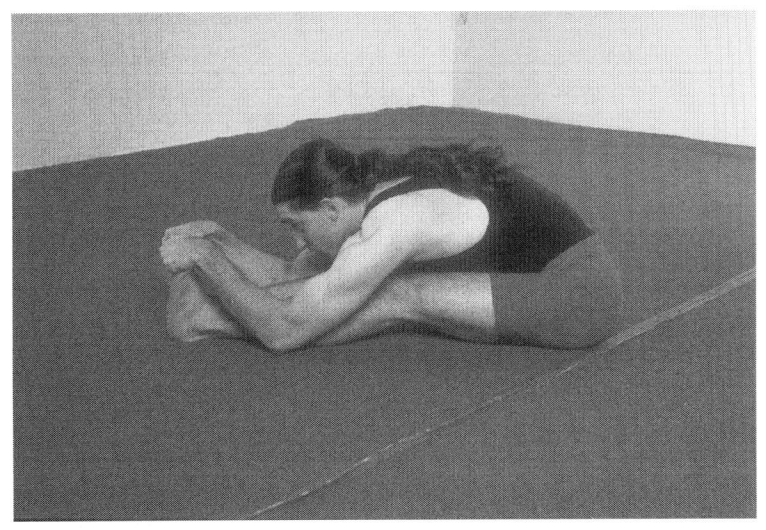

Photo 3: Continue leaning into a forward bend, holding feet if you are able, and look up.

Partner Straddle Stretch

Photo 1: Two people sitting in straddle stretch facing each other.

Photo 2: Holding hands or wrists, keeping arms straight, and leaning back one at a time.

Photo 3: The partner that is NOT leaning back allows him/her self to be 'pulled' gently as each partner supports the other as she/ he stretches.

The Downward Dog

This is a popular yoga posture that does a number of things:
1) Strengthens the arms, shoulders, abdomen, hips, thighs and back muscles.
2) Stretches the muscles, ligaments and nerves in the back of the legs.
3) Stretches, tones and strengthens the entire spinal column.

This is one of my favorite stretches to do before and after an aerial workout.

Directions:
1) Bend forward and walk hands about one length away from feet. Spread fingers wide apart.
2) Press the palms of your hands and the soles of your feet downward. Allow hips and tailbone to rise upward and feel the spine elongating.
3) Press your heels downward and feel the backs of your legs lengthening.
4) Press the crown of your head away from your shoulders. No tension in neck and shoulders.
5) To release: bend knees, walk hands in and gently roll up to standing.

Neck

Photo 1: Place hand on ear and gently pull head to side while flexing opposite hand (be sure to stretch both sides of the neck.)

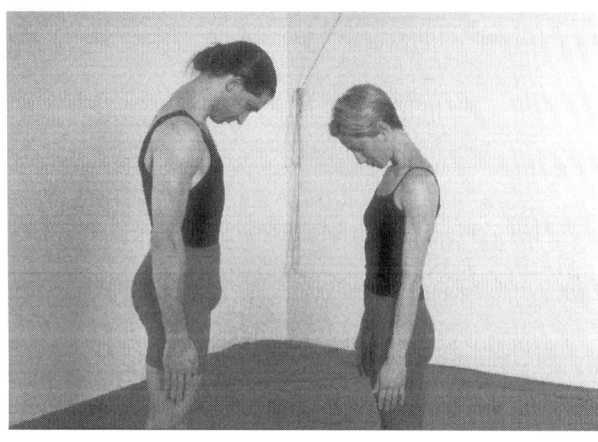

Photo 2: Drop head gently forward to stretch the back of the neck and back.

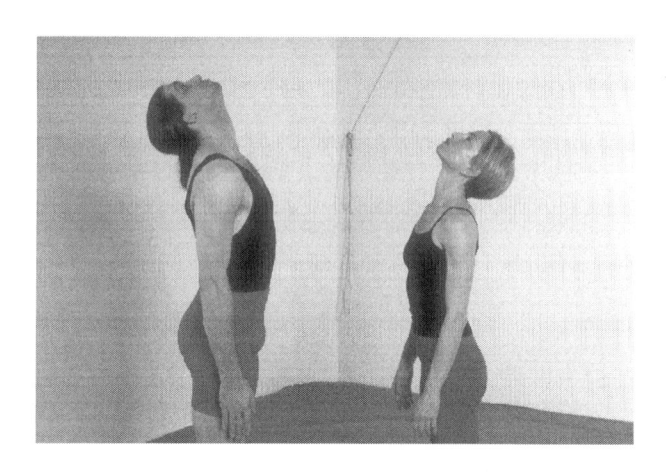

Photo 3: Rotate head gently backward to stretch the front of the neck.

Please note: If any pain is experienced in the back of the neck in this position, do not do this stretch.

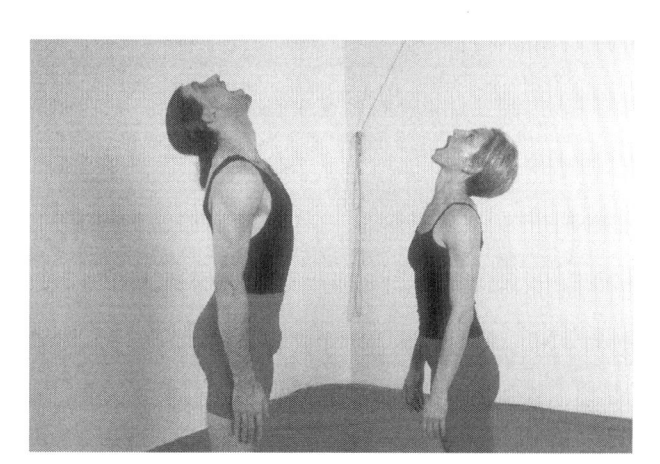

Photo 4: Open and close the mouth for an additional stretch to the front of the neck.

31

Shoulder Stretches

Never over stretch the shoulders as they are inherently unstable and if they are already flexible, you do not want to destabilize them any more. However, if your shoulders are stiff, these stretches are important tools to prevent injuries that could happen when the range of motion is challenged. Always warm up the shoulders before aerial work, but do not stretch unless shoulders have a limited range of motion, in which case you should actively work to stretch them before and after aerial work. Be sure to maintain proper scapular position, shoulder blades pulled together in back and lats pulled down with relaxed neck and trapezius muscles.

Rotator Cuff

Photo 1: Rotator cuff #1: Cross one arm straight across chest, place opposite hand above elbow and pull gently across body. Be sure to keep the shoulders pulled back, shoulder blades together, and do <u>not</u> feel like the shoulder is being pulled out of the socket.

Photo 2: Rotator cuff #2: Raise both arms over head, keeping proper shoulder position. Bend one hand behind head, place other hand on elbow and carefully pull across while gently pushing back with head. Keep scapula pulled down, do not let latissimus dorsi wing out' to the side, and do not arch your back.

Photos 3 & 4: Rotator cuff #3: Begin with both arms over head. Bring one hand around and place back of hand on back. Try to reach over head and behind back with other hand and grab fingertips. If you cannot reach, hold a towel in top hand to be grabbed by bottom hand. Be sure to keep shoulders back, not tipped forward.

Wall Shoulder Stretch

Photo 1: Stand facing wall. Place both hands flat on wall at shoulder height at least shoulders' width apart. (If you experience pinching, place hands farther apart.) Lower shoulders to below level of hands, keeping abs engaged, and try to press shoulders closer to the wall. Keep head in line with spine, and shoulders in correct position, scapulae pulled towards each other and lats pulled towards waist.

Photo 2: Another person can assist by putting gentle pressure on the shoulder blades of the other person.

Cobra

Photo 1: Lie flat on tummy, hands beside armpits, palms facing down. Engage abdominals muscles by drawing them into the spine.

Photo 2: Press up.

Photo 3: Continue pressing up until elbows are straight. Arch back and look upward.

Child's Pose

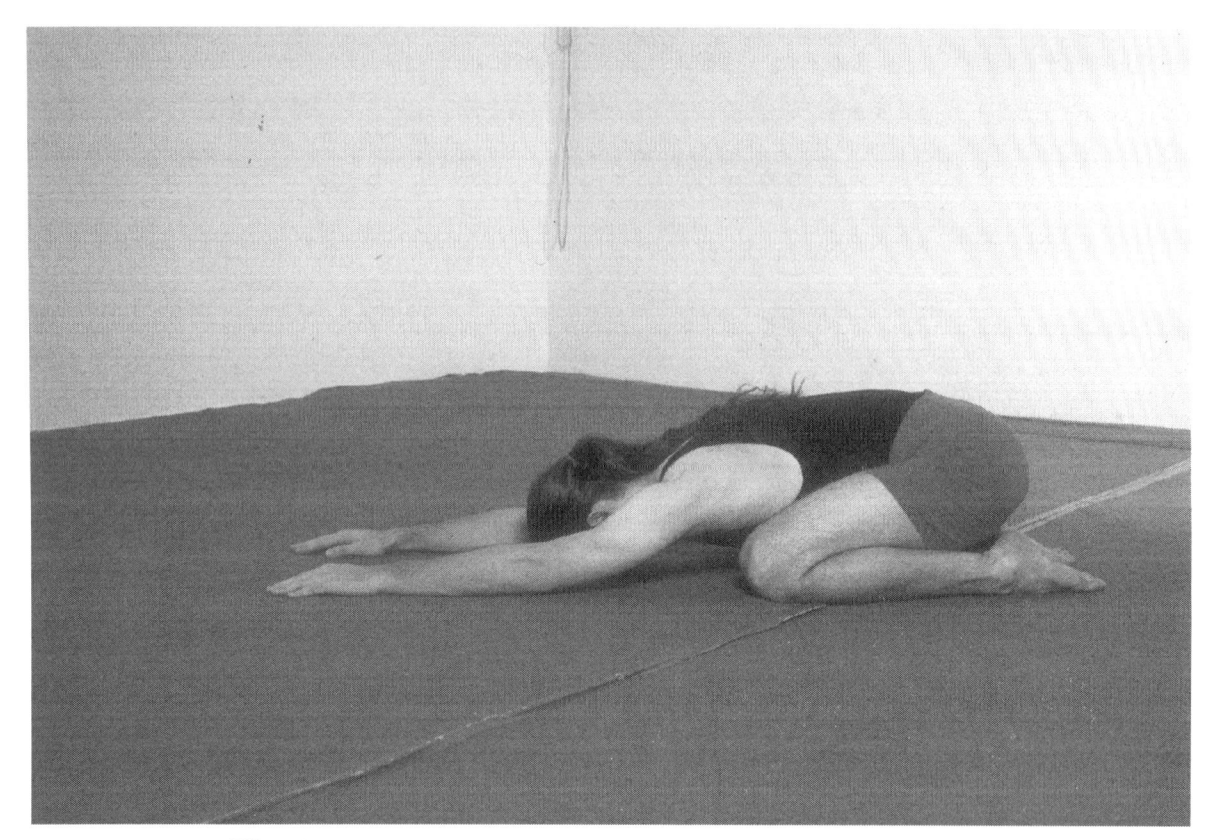

Photo: Feet are close together, knees are open and palms are flat on the floor with arms exended and elbows touching the floor. Sit back onto heels and place forehead on ground.

Back Bend

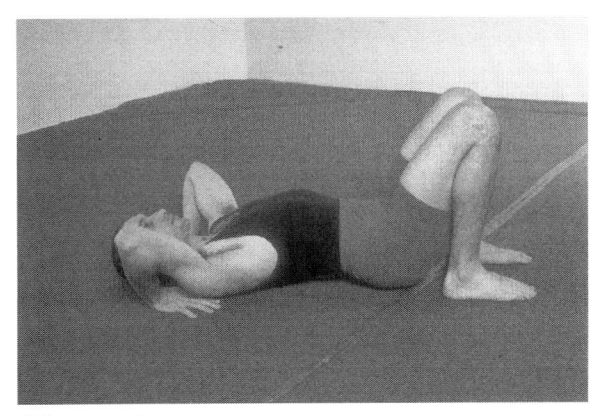

Photo 1: Begin by lying flat on back with knees bent and feet flat on floor. Place hands just below ears with palms to the floor and fingers pointing toward feet. Engage abdominals muscles by drawing them into the spine.

Photo 2: Gently press up with hands and feet aiming tummy toward the sky.

Photo 3: Continue pressing upward into *Back Bend* position.

Photo 4: Once in the *Back Bend*, you may straighten legs for increased stretch.

Photo 5: To come out of *Back Bend*, bend elbows and knees and slowly lower body to the floor. Gently lift head and neck to lead body out of *Back Bend*.
Alternatively, you may have a spotter assist you in coming up to standing position.

Standing Back Bend

Photo 1: From a standing position, look up at hands. Engage abdominals muscles by drawing them into the spine.

Photo 2: Arch back leading with arms.

Photo 3: Continue arching back, engaging abdominal muscles, until you reach the floor.

Photo 4: Once in the *Back Bend*, you may straighten legs for increased stretch.

Note to Spotter: Be sure to bend knees and use leg muscles rather than back (keep back straight) when spotting.

Trapeze

PLEASE NOTE: In some cases, spotters in this manual are positioned a step or two away from the student for the photographic needs of this manual. The position and how to spot is indicated by the photo; however, please note that it is necessary to be CLOSE enough to your student so that you can properly spot and catch them on all occasions. Consequently, when viewing the position of the spotters, be advised that it will be necessary (in most cases) for you to take a step or two CLOSER to your student on the equipment so that you can spot them with greater ease. As a spotter you must have your hands on the student whenever they are doing a new trick.

DISCLAIMER:
In doing any aerial trick there is a real chance of injury no matter how "safe" or experienced you are and no matter who is spotting or teaching you. The author, or anyone else whose advice was used in writing this manual, will not be responsible for any injury or misunderstanding resulting from the practice or performance of any feats described in this work-which includes every single page and movement seen in this manual. Purchase or use of this document constitutes agreement of this effect. Furthermore, the author does not use or discuss safety lines in this document. The author advises consulting a professional rigger when it comes to using any safety lines or hanging equipment.

I. Equipment

Trapezes vary in types, shapes and sizes. Most static and swinging trapeze are either stainless steel or chrome-plated solid bars. Some teachers use wooden bars. The bar is approximately ¾ inch to 1 inch in diameter and 1 foot 9 inches to 25" in length, however some are longer or there may be more bar on the outside of the rope especially if used for a doubles act. The diameter and length of the bar will be based on your personal preference. The standard way to measure a single trapeze bar for proper fit is to sit down with one fist on either side of your hips. Take the measurement from the outside of your fists. This is the bar length that you need.

There are several ways to make trapezes.
1. This method was originally intended for swinging trapeze. In this method, the weld goes all the way around. The basic description is as follows: After determining your rope size, (for example 1" twist, or 3 strand), you need 2, 1" thimbles. The bar itself fits thru the thimbles. After you fit the thimbles on (thru) each end of the bar, weld the thimbles to the bar all the way around. Then the rope is spliced around the thimbles.
In this way the thimbles support the bar even before it's welded. It becomes one solid piece and after the ropes are spliced on, there is never any play in your bar. For swinging trapeze some like to thread cable thru the rope and around.
2. Double Eye Trapeze Bar: Have 'loops' welded onto both sides and attach ropes threaded through the eyes and have thimbles on either end of the rope. In this method there is more play in your bar.
3. There are other trapezes that do not have 'loops' on the ends where the ropes are directly attached to or wrapped around the bar.

When using welds, cover the welds on the bar with foam of some sort wrapped with duct tape, and then cover the foam with a cloth covering.
There are many kinds of rope to use: polyester (double esterlon rope is one type), cotton or blends. If you cover your ropes (often a good idea if using polyester), it is important to get a fabric that is strong and not slippery. Wash fabric before covering. Plain cotton ropes usually do not require a cloth covering.
Heavy duty carabiners can be attached to the top thimbles to be used to rig the trapeze from the hang point.

Regardless of which trapeze you choose to use, it is important that someone who knows how to make a trapeze be the one to construct it for you.

1) You, as the teacher or performer, are responsible for your own safety and therefore responsible for the upkeep and maintenance of your equipment.
2) If you use welds on your trapeze, you must have the welds checked regularly by a professional rigger. (If you cover your welds, then you must open up and remove the covering to properly check them).
3) Welds should be checked at least every 2 years and more often if the trapeze is exposed to high moisture environments or conditions. The ropes, as well as the splices, must also be checked by a professional rigger at least every 2 years. If your equipment is made of steel, it should be chrome-plated to keep the steel from rusting when exposed to moisture. Perspiration contains moisture and salts which attack bare metal and could even cause equipment failure and personal injury.

There are a growing number of specialized companies and individuals who now produce many varieties of trapezes. A good reference is Hovey Burgess' book ***Circus Techniques*** first published in 1976 and reprinted in 1983 and revised in 1989 by Brian Dube. The appendix contains information on making your own equipment, but if you are unsure of anything, consult a professional. There are many professional circus people and equipment builders with precise knowlege and extensive experience. One such company is Custom Built Equipment, they can be reached at 937-372-7581, website cbe-circus.com and e-mail cbei@cbe-circus.com. There are many other sources of equipment, Custom Built is one of the many. Several others include www.Barry.ca, www.unicycle.fr, www.Bobbysbigtop.com

II. Instructor Notes

Photo 1

Photo 2

GENERAL (Also applies for other equipment)

1. Always wrap thumbs (unless you determine child's hand is too small to do this or they resist doing it consistently). It is necessary to repeat this every single time a child holds onto the bar and does not wrap their thumbs.
2. Instructor/spotter places their hand(s) over and around student's hand(s) to help support them whenever indicated. This is often necessary with small children when they are first beginning on the trapeze.
3. Help steady trapeze for the child.
4. Having physical contact with student even when they are not doing a "trick" is often necessary. You can use your intuition on this for each individual student; for example, for someone who has never been more than 4 feet off the ground due to a fear of heights- it is necessary and reassuring for them to have your hand(s) on their legs when they are sitting on the trapeze...or for you to have your hands on their feet when they are first learning to stand up. It is never a bad idea to say something like "I will be placing my hands on your feet/legs, etc..." as some individuals may not feel as comfortable as others with being touched.
5. Keep a watchful eye out for points of contact; a student's hands around bar, rope or rings, as well as feet and/or legs. Help prevent slipping by having students come out of trick and rest or by assisting/holding them where ever necessary.
6. Master a trick still before attempting to do it swinging.
7. Spotters walk with student as s/he is learning a trick swinging.
8. Remember when someone is doing a trick, it is difficult at first for this student to hold the trick for too long, so instruct them to do the trick then come out of the trick and rest for a moment. On the same note, students can not take in very much information when they are IN THE PROCESS of doing a trick unless they have done it often and are physically advanced, so save information (other than that which is NECESSARY at the moment) for when they are out of the trick or in a resting position or for when they come down.

9. Until a student has reached advanced level do not allow student to go off equipment backwards (skin the cat). This is tempting for most kids to do, but it is cautioned in Circus class because there is a high potential for shoulder injury if it is not done correctly. Just like any other "trick" that is done "incorrectly"(which means the way in which it was done is indicative of high potential for injury) the student is asked to get back up on equipment and "come down with legs in front". It is important NOT to tell a student that is "WRONG" --there is no right or wrong here. It is simply that we teach the safest methods here and explain the best you can to a student why. Experienced students may skin the cat if you feel they can do so.
10. Support student under the legs (if necessary) when getting up and/or getting down. Instruct student to come down slowly off trapeze especially if arm strength is weak.
11. Much of rope work can also be done from the sitting position.
12. Learn ALL tricks on both sides of the body. (Body Balancing).
13. Spotter can kneel or stand whichever is the best position to safely spot a student.

Photo 1: Spotter supports student under one leg by simply holding leg.

Photo 2: Student pulls up and hooks other leg.

Photo 3: Spotter supports student under both legs on the way down.

Proper Body Position

Elsie Smith & Serenity Smith Forchion are identical twins specializing in aerial acrobatics. The twins choreograph for circus, dance & theater and offer workshops and residencies to circus schools, dance companies and performers. They have taught and performed with many well known companies including a 4 year tour on Cirque du Soleil's Saltimbanco, as well as Ringling Bros. & Barnum & Bailey Circus, the New Pickle Circus, Pilobolus, the Actor's Gym, Circus Juventus, Umo Ensemble, Circus Smirkus, Air Dance Bernesconi, University of GA CORE Dance Company, Sea World San Antonio & Canopy Aerial Dance Studio. In 2003 they founded NIMBLE ARTS, their Vermont based trapeze & circus school that transitioned into the New England Center for Circus Arts in 2007. The two continue to teach at NECCA and work as Artistic Director and Executive Director of the growing school. They also have an active performing career, and have received a Special Award at the China Wuqiau Internat'l Circus Festival and the Bronze Medal at the 1st Internat'l Festival de Circo en Albacete, Spain.

In the following pages, Serenity and Elsie share a small part from their full course on proper body alignment and positions.

To find out more about this highly recommended course and the New England Center for Circus Arts please visit www.necenterforcircusarts.org or you can e-mail them at info@necenterforcircusarts.org

To find out more about Nimble Arts please visit www.nimblearts.org, and www.trapezetwins.com

> Proper shoulder position: Hang with shoulders pulled down towards waist, and shoulder blades pulled together in back. Never release this position during aerial work because the result is loose hanging on susceptible rotator cuff muscles. This can result in potential injury to the small rotator cuff muscles. Additionally, potential injury from sudden or long-term aggravation can occur. See photos on next page.

Head position: In general, the head should follow the natural line of the spine. When upright and hanging from the bar, ears should be between arms, chin lifted a little, as if a string were pulling up from the center of the top of the head. In other positions, for example, when back is arched, head should follow the spine shape, not flop backward or jut forwards out of line.

Core Alignment & Abdominal Position: To establish the proper alignment of the body, remember the natural curves of the spine and maintain this position by engaging the stabilizing abdominal muscles to hold body in place. Think of keeping the rib cage pulled down to the navel and lower abs flattened towards the back without losing the small natural curve of the lower back, and the side (oblique) abs contracted to hold body in place. The abs must always be engaged and pulled in towards the spine to flatten the stomach and provide stability and connection for the entire body. When the abs are not engaged, it disrupts the position of the body and prevents the shoulders and back from working correctly, thus risking injury. The abs should never be pushed out like a potbelly, and the abs should never be fully relaxed during any trapeze position (or for that matter any work out or even daily activities). Note: the abs work like an elastic band. They must stay engaged during movement including backwards arching in order to keep the body connected, but you must allow them to stretch in order to have the range.

Photo 1: Example of proper body position.

Photo 2: Example of improper body position.

Photo 3: Example of proper body position.

Photo 4: Example of improper body position.

46

The Beat

Photos 1, 2 & 3: Hang under the bar maintaining proper shoulder position. Contract lower abs to slightly swing hips and toes forward, then swing legs backward and forward again in an increasingly larger arc using kinetic momentum. Keep head in line with body. Movement should be smooth and controlled but not stiff or loose. In the front, try to lift abs and hips up to the ceiling to achieve a flat body position parallel to the ground. In the back swing, keep legs straight and together and increase the arch by activating the back muscles.

The Pull-Over

Photos 1, 2, 3 & 4: From *The Beat* come up and over the bar to the *Pull-Over*.

48

III. Tricks

Trapeze tricks 01-08 make up The First Lesson.

I recommend that all beginning students start with a basic set of tricks, which I call The First Lesson to become acquainted with being on the trapeze. Once the student is comfortable with these tricks, the instructor should introduce them to the other tricks in this manual, matching difficulty of the trick to the level of the student's ability.

T01. Hang on Bar

Practice hanging in Proper Body Position under the trapeze. This allows you to get used to holding onto the trapeze and begin strength building.

Photo 1: Tucking into the "Egg under the Bar" position

Photos 2 & 3: Explore different shapes with the legs while hanging extending and splitting the legs as seen in this photo.

T02. Hook Knees on Bar and the Knee Hang

Stand facing the bar and place hands on bar with thumbs wrapped as always. Kick feet up and tuck and pull bent knees into chest. Feet must go under bar first, then pull with arms to bring feet over top of bar. (Note: some students may need to kick feet up and over the bar. Some students may need help from spotter to do this as photographed in The Trapeze Instructor notes). Hook knees securely over the bar and keep hands holding onto bar.

Photo 1: Hook Knees on Bar. Start from knees hooked on bar. Spot the student's shins to make sure knees stay securely over bar. Check to make sure thumbs are wrapped.

In this drawing, the hips are tight which is hard on the hip flexors, and causes many back problems in aerialists.

Photo 2: The Knee Hang. Student lets go with hands and hangs down. (Spotter has hands over student's shins).

In this drawing the hips are more open and balanced. This is the precursor to proper hip position in ankle hang and many duo tricks.

Don't push down too much on feet unless necessary or student won't learn to hold on with legs by themselves.

T03. Sitting on the Bar

Photo 1: Start from knees hooked on bar.

Photo 2: Grab a rope with one hand.

Photo 3: Then grab the second rope with the other hand.

Photo 4: Pull self up to sitting.

T04. Sitting Lay Back

Photo 1: From a seated position on the bar, grab the ropes at waist level. Gently lean back until the arms are straight. Arch the back and point the toes.

Photo 2: Foot to knee.

Photo 3: Extend leg straight up for style.

Foot to Bar

If student is not ready to stand up on the trapeze bar, experiment with (while sitting) bending one knee and placing the foot of the bent knee on the bar. Repeat with the other foot. Continue this practice until student is ready to move on to standing.

T05. Standing Up

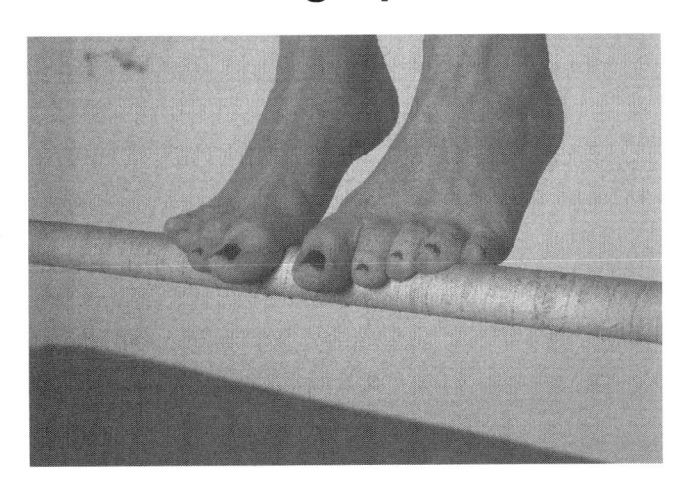

Photo 1: Stand on balls of feet with heels as high as possible. This keeps the hips and ankles aligned over the bar and makes balance and moving easier.

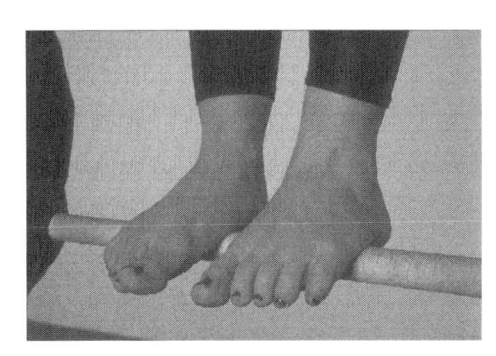

Photo 2: Standing on the arches of feet is NOT recommeded as it becomes a bad habit that is hard to break.

T06. Balancing with Feet

Photo 1: Foot to knee.    **Photo 2:** Foot in front.    **Photo 3:** Foot in back.

Remember to Body Balance and do the same with the other foot.

T07. Squat

Photo: Squat with two feet on bar while bending both knees.

T08. The Cradle aka Bird's Nest
(End of the First Lesson)

Photo 1: Start with knees hooked securely over the bar and keep hands on bar.

Photo 2: With hands still on bar and thumbs wrapped, hook ankles on or just above the padded part of the ropes.

Photo 3: Push hips through your elbows, arch your back and flex your feet to keep them secure against the ropes.

Come out of the Cradle by reversing the arch **(Photo 2)** and returning to knees over the bar **(Photo 1)**. Come down by bringing feet under the bar.

54

T09. The L-Up aka Rock & Roll

The L aka Pike

Before you start: Try the *L* aka *Pike:* Position body in a pike under the bar while hanging by your hands.

The L-Up

Photo 1: Bring the legs up as if into a knee hang but instead of falling back into a knee hang, grab the ropes one hand at a time. Students may prefer to hold higher on the ropes than demonstrated in this photo; this is personal preference.

Photo 2: Straighten the legs under the bar into a pike position and feel the bar on the back of the legs where you want to sit on it.

Photo 3, 4, & 5: Shoot legs/hips/torso straight up and over the bar.

NOTE: When performing the L-Up swinging, it is easiest to go into the "L" in the front of the swing and to sit up in the back of the swing. In this way, you are using the natural force of the swing to your greatest advantage.

T10. Swing while sitting

Photos 1 & 2: Two legs together while swinging forward.

OR

Photo 3: One knee bent while swinging backwards.

Photo 4: Two knees bent while swinging backwards.

T11. Side Lay Back

Photo 1: Begin by sitting slightly sideways with inside leg bent, and knee up against side of trapeze, and outside

Photos 2 & 3: Lean body back in the direction of the straight leg, while holding on to the same rope with both hands.

Photo 4: Take one hand off rope and extend arm to style. You can then put that hand back on and take off other hand (not shown).

Photo 5: With hand that is extended, hold foot or, if you are flexible enough, touch foot to head as seen above.

NOTE TO SPOTTER: In **Photos 1 & 2,** *spotter's hand is over student's extended leg. This is a good spotting technique to maintain throughout the entire trick not only to have more contact with student who might be fearful of leaning back, but also as a more cautious approach to spotting which is recommended for beginners.*

T12. Leg-Up Side Lay Back aka Star variation

Photo 1:
With two hands on the same rope, sit slightly sideways with inside leg straight up on the opposite rope. Hook your big and next toe onto this rope and extend the other leg straight down.

Photo 2:
Variation known as "Star" can be done here where hips are turned toward ceiling and instep of foot is on the rope; either hand can be removed!

Photo 2:
Straighten arms and begin to lay back as you rotate hips forward so hip is resting on bar.

Photo 3:
Release bottom hand, open body and style.

T13. Splits

Photo 1: Start with both knees and hands on the bar. Remove one leg from bar, move it to below bar and extend.

NOTE: You can also start with foot on the bar (not pictured) to aid the push into full splits. This is also the way it is taught for the flying trapeze.

Photo 2: Beat up with bottom leg.

Photo 3: Then beat down.

Photo 4:
& Then beat up.

Photo 5:
Then kick into the *Split*. NOTE: for flying or easier position for fixed trapeze, the back of the thigh is rested on the bar (not pictured).

Photo 6:
Bend front knee and do a *Stag*.

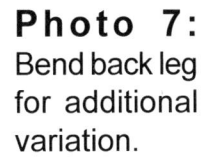

Photo 7:
Bend back leg for additional variation.

60

T14. Standing Up Gracefully

Photos 1 & 2: From sitting, place hands at ear height, shift back to above knees.

Photo 3: Sit up straight (which gives the illusion that you are sitting on your behind).

Photo 4: Go into one foot sqaut, and point straight leg toward ground. NOTE: Spotter can hold ankle to aid balance and keep connection.

Photo 5: Reach up and hold very high on ropes. NOTE: A lot of people miss this step and then feel very off-balanced as they stand. This is an important step for balance and aesthetics.

Photos 6, 7 & 8: Stand up and do a foot-to-knee style. NOT PICTURED: As soon as you are standing move hands up to ear height for easier position.

T15. Double-Legged Cradle
(or Bird's Nest)

T16. 1/4 Angel
aka One Legged Bird's Nest

Photo: From a cradle position, put both feet on one side of the rope.

Photos 1 & 2: From the cradle position, one foot is taken off and dropped toward the ground. Spotter might want to move to other side as other leg is extended if this feels safer.

T17. Standing Lay Back

Photo: From a standing position on the bar, grab the ropes at shoulder height, lean gently back, straighten the arms and look back.

Not photographed: Practice balancing with one foot off bar.

T18. The Egg (Preparation for Cradle on the Ropes)

Photo 1: From a standing position on the bar, holding ropes at shoulder height, inhale then exhale as you lift feet off trapeze bringing knees up.

NOTE: After the student can hold this position for 10 or more seconds, he is usually ready to try a cradle on the ropes.

Photo 2: Do the Egg and then tilt body slightly backwards and look back with head.
This can serve as an interim step if the student is not yet ready to do complete cradle on the ropes.

NOTE TO SPOTTER: It is very important to make sure student has enough strength to support his/her own body weight, with energy to spare, before proceeding to aerial activity on the ropes. If student has not yet completed the 10-second preparation for a Cradle on the Ropes (The Egg), then continue practicing this until student has increased strength, then come back to cradle on the ropes later. Spotter can also 'steady' the trapeze for the student as s/he lifts up into the egg for the first time and place bar beneath their feet as they come out of the position.

T19. Cradle on the Ropes aka Bird's Nest on Ropes

Prerequisite: *Cradle on the Bar* (T08).

Photo 1: From a standing position on the bar, grab the ropes at about shoulder high. NOTE: This can also be done from sitting on the bar if student or spotter are uncomfortable (see instructor notes #11).

Photo 2: Pull the body up into a tuck where the shins are facing the sky.

Photo 3: Then hook your ankles on the ropes.

NOTE TO SPOTTER: It is best to spot the student from the back of the trapeze as most of the student's body will be behind the bar. Also be prepared to put the bar under feet as student comes out of position.

Photo 5: *Cradle on the Ropes* with straight legs.

Photos 5 & 6: Arch the back and look up (as done in *Cradle on the Bar*). Two different styles are shown.

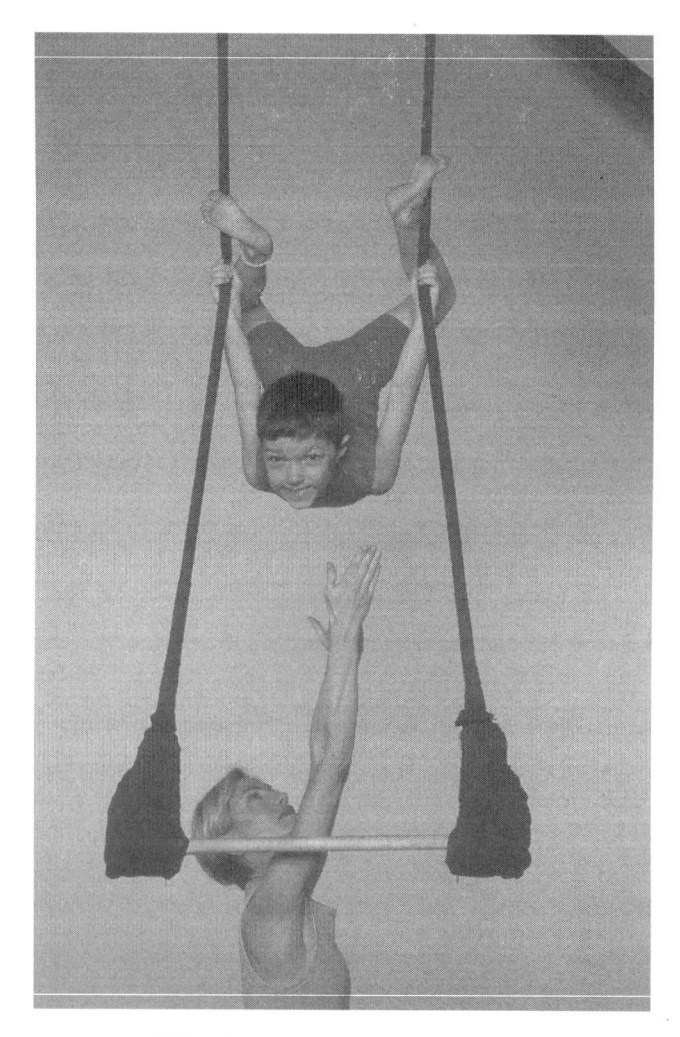

Photo 6: *Cradle on the Ropes* with bent knees.

T20. Squat Routine

Photo 1: Squat with feet on bar holding ropes with hands.

Photo 2: Straighten one leg in front.

Photo 3: Place straight leg behind bar.

T21. Standing Swing-Basic technique

NOTE: Do not do this without a safety line until your instructor says you are ready to do so.

Photos 1, 2, 3 & 4: Pumping forward as you bend the knees and straighten them in a wave motion. Hands at ear height.

Photos 5 & 6: Pumping backwards bending the knees and straightening.

Photo 7 & 8: Pumping forward extending one leg.

NOTE: There are other techniques for swinging oneself standing not shown in this manual... especially those for advanced performers.

68

T22. Squat to Air Split

Photo 1: Squat.

Photo 2: Raise arms up rope until elbows are straight.

Photo 3: Straighten one leg in front.

Photos 4 & 5: Place straight leg behind bar, then straighten other leg with foot on bar creating an "Air Split" as you arch back. Two different styles are shown. one tilting head back

Photo 4: *Air Split* with head looking back.

Photo 5:. *Air Split* looking straight ahead.

69

T23. Rainbow Split aka Straddle

Photo 1: Stand facing the bar, hands are toward the middle, close together. Pull legs up toward bar.

Photo 2: Open legs into straddle under bar. The same trick is done here with slightly different styles.

Come out of the *Rainbow Split* by bringing knees to rest on bar or reverse the process in **Photo 1**.

T24. Pull-Over from Standing on the Ground

Photo 1: Stand facing the bar with hands spread apart holding bar.

Photos 2, & 3: Kick feet up and over and put hips over the bar.

From the *Pull Over*, you can go into the *Front Balance with Hands* and then the *Front Balance* OR you can go into the *Dolphin*.

OR

T25. Front Balance with Hands

Photo 4: From *Pull-Over*, lift upper body and support self with hands on bar.

T26. Front Balance

Photo 5: Find your balance point and release hands to balance.

T27. Dolphin

Photo 6: From *Pull-Over*, hold the ropes above the padding, thumbs facing in.

Photo 7: Lift upper body as you move hands higher up the rope.

Photo 8: Arch and look up.

71

T28. Catcher's Hang aka Catcher's Lock

Photo 2: Same as **Photo 1**, but seen from the other side.

Photo 1: Stand facing the bar, hands are toward the middle, close together. Kick legs up and over the front of the bar and open up legs wide bracing legs between ropes and bar. Abdominals are tight.

Photos 3 & 4: Bend your knees so they lock into the ropes catching behind the knees. Toes must be pointed as this helps tighten lock into place. When secure, let go with the hands.

Photo 5: Hold feet with hands as an additional trick.

Note: If you are holding someone else's weight, be sure to have proper positioning: engage the abs and pull lats towards waist, shoulder blades back and together.

72

T29. Rock & Roll Up aka Knee Hang Beat

Photo 1 : Start with both knees hooked on bar and hands holding either ropes or bar. Pull body up and prepare to 'swing' downward.

Photos 2, 3, & 4: Release hands and swing down through the knee hang position and (beat) your torso back then forward and let the momentum lift you up.

Photo 5: Grab the ropes just above the padding. (Spotter: be sure to instruct student to press down with knees and point toes. Additionally, spotter be sure to watch knees here, especially if student is doing trick with a swing).

The Next Step is to:
L- Up. (See T09).

73

T30. Single Knee Roll Up aka One Leg Russian Roll, aka One Leg Monkey Roll

Photo 1: With one knee hooked on the bar bring your elbows under the bar and your forearms up as you grab the inside of the ropes with your hands.

Photo 2: Beat up

Photo 3: Beat down &

Photo 4: Beat up

Beat as you do to get into a split

Photos 5, 6 & 7: With the help of the momentum of your last beat up, pull yourself up to sitting. Keep the knee that is hooked on bar bent and body tucked with your chin in until end of trick.

Come out of the *Single Knee Roll Up* by changing hand position one arm at a time; then bring bottom leg through to front OR after unwrapping arms, drop down into a *Single Knee Hang* (T86). (Reminder: practice this on BOTH legs to body balance).

T31. Twisting Lay Back aka Mermaid aka Fish

Photo 1: From a sitting position in the center of the bar, hold up high on the rope with right hand and take left hand off rope. Style with left arm straight out from body and behind the swing.

Photo 2: Draw left arm toward the head while person's body twists as she is leaning back so that the whole body twists towards left arm.

Reminder: As with all tricks, repeat this trick on opposite side to properly balance the body.

T32. Roll-Over aka Foot Flag

Photo 1: Sitting sideways on bar, hold rope with both hands above head (thumbs pointing down unless planning to do Roll Thru T33). Hook ankels on bottom of rope where it meets the bar.

Photo 2: Secure ankles against padding and begin to roll over.

Photo 3: Continue to roll so body hangs off bar supported by hands holding ropes and ankle(s) resting on rope/bar connection.

To come out of *Roll-Over*, reverse the process. Some find it easier if you keep your legs straight until you sit back on bar.

T33. Roll-Through

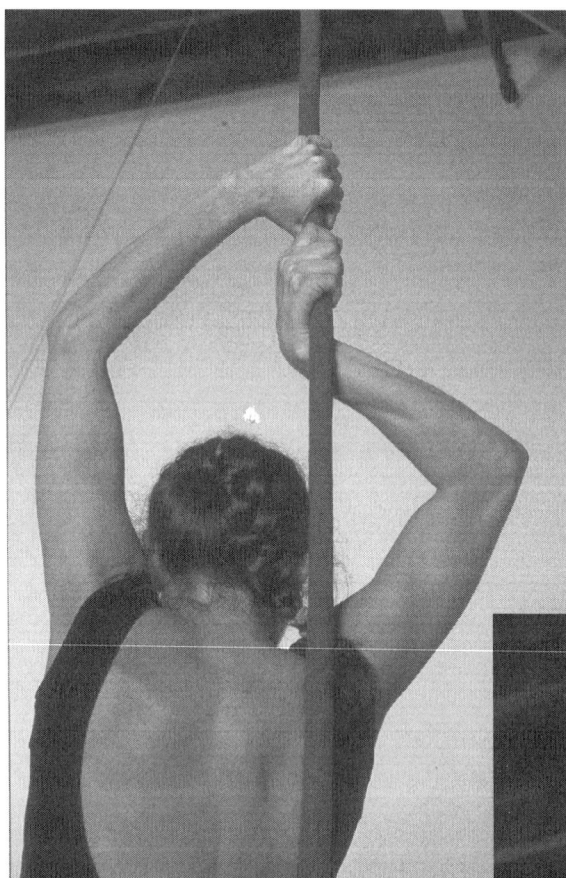

Photos 1 & 2: Sitting sideways on bar, hold rope with both hands above head. thumbs are almost touching. The top hand simply holds the thumb facing down. The wrist of the bottom hand twists around the rope with the thumb facing up.

NOTE: When the right hand is on the bottom, you roll to the right. When the left hand is on the bottom, you roll to the left.

Roll-Through

Photo 1: Sit with one leg on either side of the rope. Bend right knee and press right ankle against padding.

Photo 2: Bend left knee and secure left ankle against padding to prepare for *Roll-Through*.

Photo 3: Roll body to the right and release right leg down into a style position while holding rope with hands.

Photo 4 & 5: Continue turning body to the right and pull body in toward bar by pulling arms and by bending right leg in to meet the left leg.

Photos 6 & 7: Use arms to pull body into a sitting position on bar.

Reminder: Practice this trick on the left side also!

78

... AND...Style

T34. Crescent Moon

Photo 1: Sit on bar holding hands low on ropes.

Photo 2: Lay back

Photo 3: Extend leg up into a split positon above the bar suspending self off the bar.

T35. Bird Hang

Prerequisite: *Crescent Moon(T34).*

Photo 1: Allow the back leg to drop toward the rope it is closest to while the other knee bends to wrap the same rope.

Photo 2: Release the hand which is on the side where the legs are.

Photo 3: Release the other hand and style to do the *Bird Hang*.

81

Photo 4: To come out of the *Bird Hang*, hold the bar with both hands.

Photo 5: Release the legs and bring them under the bar as you support the body with the arms and engage the abs.

Photo 6: Move into the *Rainbow Split(T23)* to dismount and come down.

T36. Back Walk-Over

Photo 1: Begin by sitting on bar holding hands low on ropes. (IF YOU SMILE REALLY BIG, THE TRICK WILL BE EASIER!)

Photo 2: Go into a lay back.

Photo 3: Keep one leg straight and bend knee of other leg for an optional style pose.

Photo 4: Hook one foot on the rope. At this point you can bend free leg while arching back into a backbend position and style.

Photo 5: After hooking foot on rope, straighten both legs.

Photo 6: In one continuous motion, bring the free leg up, through the ropes and down into a *1/4 Angel (T16)* position. This is a slight variation to the *1/4 Angel (T16)* as hands hold onto ropes intead of the bar.

NOTE: The Back Walk-Over can also be done from a Crescent Moon position. Remember to practice with opposite foot hooked on rope.

83

T37. 1/2 Angel aka Angel 2

Photos 1 & 2: *1/2 Angel:* From the cradle, remove one hand from bar and unhook the opposite foot. Drop both toward ground while extending arm and leg in opposite directions. Look toward the hand of the extended arm.

1/2 Angel shown here on both sides of body.

Photo 3 & 4: *Inversion:* To invert, bring the extended leg and extended arm in towards center of body into a tuck.

T38. 1/2 Angel Inversion aka Angel 3

Photo 5: Turn over so tummy is facing the sky and untuck into inverted extension.
An alternative way to get into this trick is from the knee hang where you hook one foot onto rope at the ankle and remove that same hand from bar. Then extend the free leg under the bar and untuck into the inverted position.

Note: It is recommended that you flex the foot that is pressed against the rope. Some prefer to sickle the foot as demonstrated here, but please note that this technique is often less secure.

Photo 6: Instead of hooking ankle, simply rest knee over the bar.

Reverse the process to return to ½ angel postion.

85

T39. Open Angel

Photos 1 & 2: From the inverted ½ Angel (T37) position, switch hands on bar so that the hand on bar corresponds to the foot on the rope. (In this case, right hand and right foot). Grasp bar with both palms facing forward.

NOTE: Pay special attention to warming up knees before doing this trick.

Photo 3: Release left hand and extend arm into *Open Angel*.

NOTE: An alternative is to rest knee over bar instead of wrapping ankle around the rope. (In this case the right knee).

Photos 5 & 6: One way to dismount from *Open Angel* is to grasp bar again with other hand, palms facing each other, then kick into a *Rainbow Split* (T23) and dismount.

T40. Ankle Hang

You can get into the *Ankle Hang* a number of ways including, but not limited to:
1. From a *Rainbow Split (T23)*.
2. From an *Inverted 1/2 Angel (T37)* by grasping bar with both hands, and hooking the free ankle.
3. From the *Knee Hang (T02)* position, by grasping the bar with both hands then readjusting hands between the knees, as demonstrated in **Photo 1**.

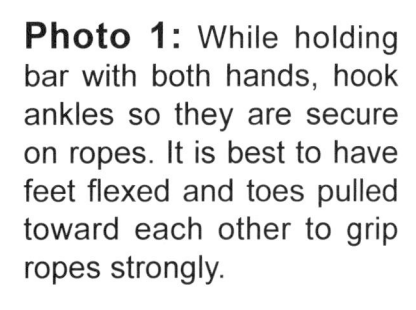

Photo 1: While holding bar with both hands, hook ankles so they are secure on ropes. It is best to have feet flexed and toes pulled toward each other to grip ropes strongly.

Photo 2: When comfortable, remove both hands from the bar and hang by ankles keeping feet flexed & toes pulled towards each other.

Photo 3: Pull up using abdominal muscles, grab bar with both hands and dismount.

You can dismount from the *Ankle Hang* by reversing any of the three starting methods described above. A fourth dismount, T41, the *Ankle Hang Dismount*, is described on the following page.

T41. Ankle Hang Dismount

NOTE: This dismount should only be attempted if you can reach the floor and if your arms can support your body weight.

Photo 1: Place your hands on the floor while in the ankle hang position.

Photo 2: Release feet and go into a handstand supporting yourself with your arms.

Photo 3, 4 & 5: Allow legs to come down one at a time, bending at the waist as you would for the last 1/2 of a back walkover.

T42. Double Knee Roll Up aka Monkey Roll onto the Bar
aka Russian Roll-Up

NOTE: This trick is one way of getting to the sitting position instead of the *"L" up (T09)*.

Photo 1: From a *Knee Hang (T02)* come into this starting position. With both knees hooked on the bar, bring your elbows under the bar and your forearms up as you grab the inside of the ropes with your hands. (Just like the *Single Knee Roll Up (T30)* but with both knees hooked on bar).

Photos 5-10: Beat down and around using the momentum of your swing to pull yourself up to sitting. Keep the knees bent and body tucked & chin in during entire roll.

Photo 2: Beat up   **Photo 3:** Beat down &   **Photo 4:** Beat up

Come out of the Double knee roll up by re-gripping arms one at a time then readjusting your seat on the bar.

T43. One Arm Stand aka Amazon

Photos 1 & 2: Closeup of starting position & full view of starting position: Begin by sitting on the bar a little sideways. Place your hand (that is on the backside of the bar) behind you on the bar with your thumb nail facing the front in between the rope and your behind. Make sure to turn your hand so that you put wrist over bar. With your other hand grab the rope over your head with the palm of your hand facing up and then into the rope. Tilt head back and place your neck on the back of the rope.

Photo 3: Next, lift your weight with top arm then slide off the bar, so your neck and the left hand (on the bar) are supporting you. Bring left hand (& bar) in front of hip.

Photo 4: Take right hand off the rope if secure.

Photos 5 - 8: Same series shown on opposite side ending with a "Foot to Knee" pose.

Note: Spotter can position self standing or kneeling as is the case with many tricks.

T44. Air Split

Photo 1: From the *One Arm Stand (T43)* pose, place outside foot (in this case, the left) up on rope and do an 'Air Split'. The inside hand (in this case right) is still holding bar and supporting the body.

Photo 2: Shows same trick on other side of bar.

T45. Sitting Air Split

Photo 1: From the *One Arm Stand (T43)* pose, sitting sideways, place inside foot (in this case the right) up on rope while neck is in *One Arm Stand (T43)* position. Lean back against rope to balance, and when secure remove right hand from bar. Extend both arms out in a style.

Photo 2: Shows same trick on other side of bar.

T46. Sitting Poses

Photo 1: Starting position from which to practice the 2 sample poses that follow.

Photo 2: Arms straight out, legs extend down. Lean forward into ropes.

These are nice poses to strike as styles in the middle of routines. They are also good poses to hold while spinning on the trapeze. For more information on spinning see T107.

Photo 3: Arms straight out, Foot to knee. Lean into ropes.

T47. Single Knee Lay Back aka Hip Hang aka Amazon aka Gazelle

Photo 1: Position yourself as if you are going into a side layback but keep the arms slightly bent.

Photo 2: Scoot your seat forward so the bar is almost at the small of your back. The balance point is different for everyone so find this spot first and then lay back slightly as you bend the inside knee. You can pull the knee toward you and hold it with the same hand if you'd like to before letting go.

Photo 3: While bending the inside knee, secure it in a position laying against the rope while keeping other leg straight.

Photo 4: Remove 'outside' hand from rope and style with arm.

Photo 5: If secure, remove other hand from rope. You can use hands to help pull free leg toward head doing contortion under bar.

*NOTE TO SPOTTER: In **Photo 1,** the spotter's hand is over student's extended leg. As noted on several occasions earlier in this manual, this is a good spotting techinique to use throughout the entire trick not only to have more contact with students who might be fearful of leaning back, but also as a more cautious approach to spotting which is recommended for beginners. In photos 2-5, the spotter has chosen to spot from a different angle for this advanced student AND so that the trick could be viewed as clearly as possible for this manual.*

T48. The Sea Horse aka Gazelle Roll-Up

Photo 1: From the *Single Knee Lay Back (T47)* position, straighten leg and prepare to hook knee.

Photo 2: Hook knee around rope.

Photo 3: Hold above rope with both hand.

Photo 4: Pull body upward.

Photo 5: Continue pulling body up as you twist toward the inside.

Photo 6:
Complete the twist so that bar rests against back rope.

Photo 7:
Straighten elbows and drop head back, neck to side of rope.

Photo 8:
Take off hands and style.

Photo 9:
Straighten leg and style.

96

T49. Star

Photo 1: From the *Back Balance (AT2)* position, grab ropes with hands, straddle legs and lean back. Adjust yourself as needed. The bar should rest in the small of your back so that you don't slip. Your thighs should rest on the ropes.

Photo 2: Let go of hands when secure.

T50. Half Bent Star

Photo 3: From the *Star*, bend one of your knees.

T51. Bent Star aka Frog Hang

Photo 4: From the *Star* bend both knees.

NOTE TO SPOTTER: The Star, Half Bent Star and the Bent Star place an added degree of pressure on the back. Make sure the student's back can support this trick. Correct form is to engage the abdominal muscles. If you are not doing this, please be aware that you risk injury.

T52. Flag

Photos 1, 2 & 3:
Sitting on the bar, wrap one arm from front to back of the ropes then grasp bar with hand.

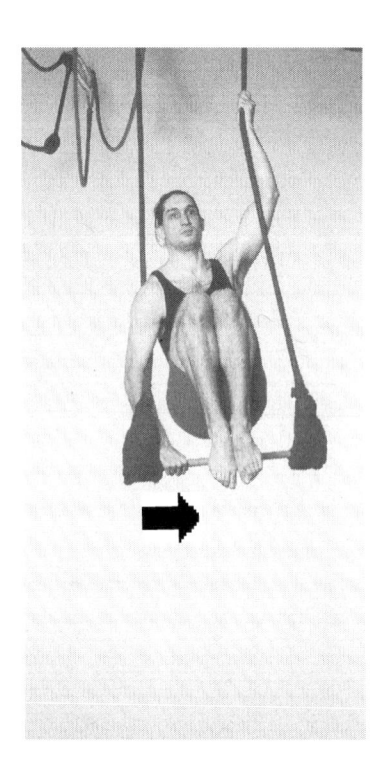

Photo 4: Lift knees up and tuck.

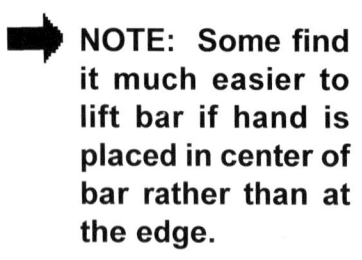

➡ **NOTE: Some find it much easier to lift bar if hand is placed in center of bar rather than at the edge.**

Photo 5: Bring legs to other side of bar and untuck.

Photo 6: Untuck and straighten legs.

Photo 7: Extend the trapeze away from body, arch back and look up.

99

T53. Double Arm Flag

Photo 1: Sitting on the bar, wrap both arms from front to back of the ropes then grasp bar with hands.

Photo 2: Using arm strength, lift body up off the bar and tuck.

Photo 3: Raise legs in a tuck and place feet on the bar.

Photo 4: Remaining in a tuck, bring legs to other side of the bar.

Photo 5: Untuck and extend legs, arch back and look up.

4. Fetal Balance

Photo 1: Sit on bar sideways with hands holding rope above head. Place one foot, then the other, on the rope you are facing. Scoot your backside towards the feet.

Photo 2: Lay back so that you are in a fetal position. Position yourself so that the rope runs between your neck and shoulder, and so that your behind is against the rope. Using your toes to hold onto the rope, bend and hug your knees.

T55. Arch Up

Prerequisite: *Fetal Balance (T54)*.

Photo 1: From the *Fetal Balance (T54)*, grasp rope with toes of one foot. Grasp rope above head, with both thumbs facing down. Place neck to side of rope. If right foot is put on rope first, then put head back on left side of rope.

Photo 2: Pull body up with arms as you grasp rope with toes of second foot above first foot.

Photo 3: Continue into an *Arch Up*.

Photo 4: Gently lower body back to the *Fetal Balance (T54)*.

102

T56. The Coffin aka Bed

Photo 1: Turn sideways on the bar and sit with back against one rope.

Photo 2: Reach over head with both hands, holding thumbs down, arms bent slightly.

Photo 3: Put toes of outside foot (the one not against the rope) onto the rope approximately at chest level. Note: depending on the width of the trapeze and the height of the person, the position of the foot on the rope will change. Put head back so rope is against neck.

Photo 4: Push on the foot to straighten out body and lift hips towards the ceiling.

103

Photo 5: Place inside foot over other foot pushing on ropes keeping straight body.

Photo 6: If stable, can release the arm that can pinch rope between neck and arm and put it straight over head in line with body. If you fall to one side this arm serves as a safety.

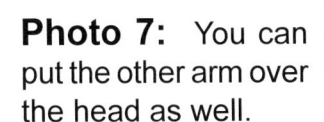

Photo 7: You can put the other arm over the head as well.

Note: The flatter the body (less arch) the easier the balance is.

Photo 8: To come down, hold rope overhead again with both hands, take second foot down, cross it under first leg and bend body to sit on bar.

T57. Scissor Sit aka Cuddle

Photos 1 & 2: While sitting on bar sideways, arm that is closest to rope extends up and is wrapped around rope from back to front grasping rope with hand up high.

NOTE: If you are scooted over to the right side, then your right arm will be the one to extend up and wrap and it will be your right leg that will 'scissor' the rope (see next page).

Photo 3: Bend knee of your corresponding wrapped arm, to prepare to 'scissor' the rope.

Photo 4: Extend bent knee as you cross it over other leg and 'scissor' the rope.

Photo 5: Bend the knee again as you sit in the *Scissor Sit* position.

Photo 6: Alternative *Scissor Sit* position with arm not wrapped.

T58. Scissor Roll

Photos 1, 2 & 3: Repeat first 3 steps of *Scissor Sit (T57)*.

Photo 4: Next roll body off bar and remove unwrapped hand.

Photo 5: Continue roll as you circle free arm around.

Photos 6 & 7: Extend free arm in a pose as you open body up, straighten legs and arch your back.

106

T59. Scissor Roll Around (demonstrated on the right side)

Photo 1: Hold rope with left hand on top of right hand and with both thumbs up.

Photo 2: Cross right leg over left leg and 'scissor' the rope.

Photo 3: While holding firmly with hands and keeping elbows bent, roll body around using left leg to secure self. Press back against rope. **This is POSITION 1**.

Photo 4: Continue to roll body around as trapeze twists upward under back and around left leg.

Photo 5: Lay back on rope as left leg is between twisted rope and extend arms. **This is POSITION 2**.

Photo 6: Hold ropes with hands and begin to pull up.

Photo 7: Pull up and arch. **This is POSITION 3**.

Photo 8: Same as **Photo 7** and bring foot to knee and style.

T60. Fall Back Cradle (prerequisite is the Cradle (T08))

Photo 1: Sitting on bar place hands on either side of behind on bar.

NOTE TO SPOTTER: Begin spot with inside hand/arm under back (In this case the right hand/arm.) For many students it is imperative that you help control the speed of their drop which will require you to put a hand (in this case the left) up high on the upper back (NOT PICTURED) to control the drop – then switch right hand to shoulders as left hand slides to belly as feet hook and cradle is formed.

Photo 2: Gently lean back opening legs wide and pushing them against ropes to slow fall.

Photo 3: Catch ropes with legs as you fall into a *Cradle (T08)*.

T61. Fall Back 1/4 Angel (prerequisite is the *Fall Back Cradle (T60)* and *1/4 Angel (T16)*

Photo 1: Sitting on bar place hands on either side of behind on bar.

NOTE TO SPOTTER: Begin spot with inside hand/arm under back (In this case the right hand/arm. Same as for Fall Back Cradle(T60).

NOTE TO SPOTTER:

As student falls back you then place outside hand/arm under belly as feet hook and cradle is formed. (In this case the left hand/arm). Same as for Fall Back Cradle (T60).

Photo 2: Gently lean back opening legs wide the same as *Fall Back Cradle (T60)* except one foot does NOT hook on rope.

Photo 3: Catch rope with one leg instead of two. The second leg is allowed to fall through into a ¼ Angel (T16).

T62. Fall Back 1/2 Angel (prerequisite is the *Fall Back 1/4 Angel (T61)* and *1/2 Angel (T37)*

Photo 1:
While sitting on bar begin with one hand on bar other on rope as a 'safety'.

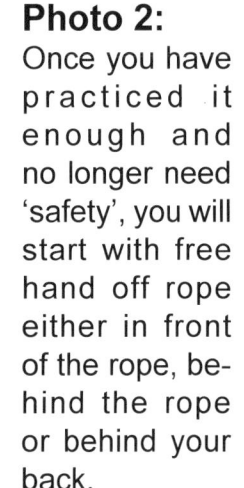

Photo 2:
Once you have practiced it enough and no longer need 'safety', you will start with free hand off rope either in front of the rope, behind the rope or behind your back.

Note to spotters: Many teachers prefer to spot on the other side for this trick so the student rolls their belly into the spotter. Although you must be aware of the leg coming toward you, this side often allows for the spotter to "spot" much sooner for this particular trick.

Photo 3:
Fall back and hook leg on rope where 'safety' hand is.

Photo 4:
Release safety when leg feels secure.

Photo 5 & 6:
Complete the 'fall' into the ½ Angel (T37) position with hand holding bar and opposite foot hooked on opposite rope. Extend free hand and leg.

NOTE TO SPOTTER: Please follow same directions as listed for Fall Back Cradle and 1/4 Angel (T60 and T61.)

T63. Dragon Fly

Photo 1: Starting position for *Dragon Fly*: while sitting on bar one arm extends up and wraps around rope from back to front grasping rope with hand up high. Other hand holds bar palm facing forward at point closest to rope.

Photo 2: Supporting self with arm up high and other hand on bar, slide off front of bar in upright position.

T64. Dragon Catcher aka Mermaid with Ankles Hooked

Photo 1: From *Dragon Fly (T63)* position, bring or beat legs up towards rope that is opposite the rope you are holding.

Photos 2 & 3: Catch rope with ankles while keeping hand on bar.

Photos 4: Release hand from bar and extend body into Dragon Catcher.

Photo 5: Another option is to release top ankle and exend leg down.

T65. Standing X

Photo: From a standing position on the bar, grab the ropes a bit above the shoulders and place the feet just above or on the padding on the ropes. Push the arms and legs straight out. Tension will hold you in an X.

T66. Standing Side Lay Back

Photo 1:
While straddling rope from outside, place one foot in front of the other on bar, hold onto rope with one hand and lay back releasing second hand as you extend into layback.

Photo 2:
Switch hands on rope and you can also switch position of feet on bar.

T67. Monkey Roll aka Forward Roll

Photos 1 & 2: From standing on the bar (on your toes), reach in front of the ropes and grab at waist level thumbs pointing down.

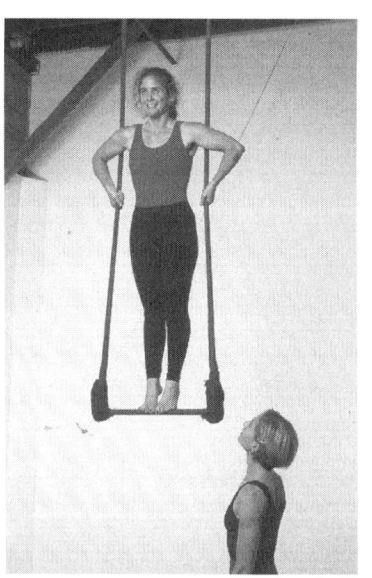

NOTE: You can also do a *Forward Roll* with your thumbs pointing up. I find this to be a little more challenging so be sure you are strong enough if you choose to try it that way.

Photos 3 & 4: Lean forward with hips staying in front of the ropes. Pike over as far as possible until arms are straight. Then the forward roll will happen automatically.

Photos 5 & 6: Raise body up slightly so that your behind lands sitting on the bar.

NOTE: To do an inverted Monkey Roll aka Back Roll, you start sitting on the bar - **(Photo 6)** *and literally reverse the steps of the Forward Monkey Roll doing a backwards roll to standing -* **(Photo 1)**. *Some switch hands to a normal grip for this, ending at Photo 2.*

T68. Arabesque Monkey Roll

Photos 1 & 2: From standing on the bar (on your toes), reach in front of the ropes and grab at waist level thumbs pointing down. This is the same starting position as for the *Monkey Roll (T67)*.

Photo 3: Keeping legs straight lift up one leg into *Arabesque AKA Lean Out*

Photos 4: Continue extending leg behind and up as you bend at the waist and lean forward while looking up and arching.

Photo 5: Let head drop as back releases arch into a forward roll.
Note: At this point you can add a *Split on the Ropes(T74)*.

Photos 6, 7 & 8: Roll forward and raise body up slightly so that your behind lands sitting on the bar. This is the same ending as *Monkey Roll (T67)*.

T69. Double Legged Cradle on the Ropes

Photo 1:
From a standing position on the bar, grab the ropes about shoulder high and pull the body up into a tuck where the shins are facing the sky.

Photo 2:
Then hook both ankles on one side of rope.

Photo 3:
Arch back and look up.

T70. 1/4 Angel on the Ropes

Prerequisite: *Cradle on the Ropes (T19)*.

Photo 1: Release one leg and bring foot to knee.

Photo 2: Extend free leg into *1/4 Angel*.

T71. Rainbow Split on the Ropes

Photo: From a standing position on the bar with arms about shoulder height, engage abs and bring legs up and straddle the rope.

T72. Straight Up & Down

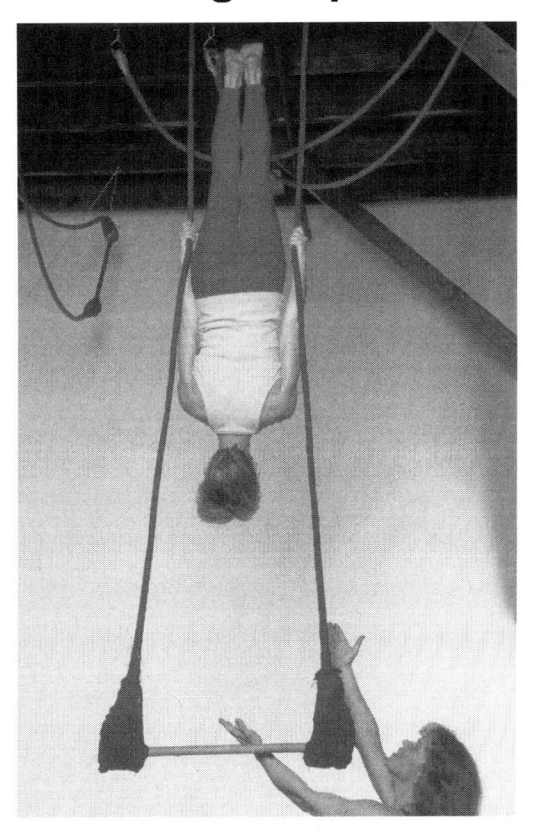

Photo: From a standing position on the bar with arms about shoulder height bring legs up as you would for a cradle on the ropes, but instead point feet straight up into the air and make the body straight like a plank. Be sure to look straight ahead so that head is not tilting up OR down but instead pointed straight.

T73. Inside Out Egg

Photo 1:

From a *Straight Up & Down (T72)*, bring feet toward head while arching back and tilting head toward feet.

T74. Split on the Ropes

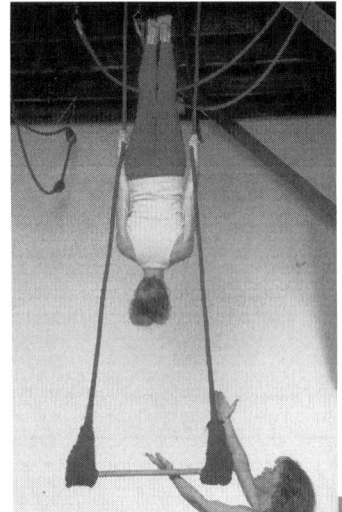

Prerequisite: *Straight Up and Down (T72)*

Photo: From the *Straight Up & Down (T72)* open legs into a *Split*, gently arching back and tilting head toward back.

T75. Freedman Flag

Photo 1: Standing sideways on the bar hold with two hands on one rope; inside elbow behind the rope. Place one foot, at about shoulder height on opposite rope, using toes to secure.

Photo 2: Pull up with arms, place second foot using toes to secure above or below first foot.

Photo 3: Press hips up toward the sky and straighten legs so that body is parallel to the bar.

T76. Sitting Lay Back on the Ropes

Photo 1: Standing on bar, place one hand above head on rope and other hand below shoulders on other rope.

Photo 2: Pull legs up, one on each side of the rope where the hand is held below the shoulder.

Photo 3: Sit on lower hand and straighten legs while pulling up slightly with other hand and pressing hips up toward the sky.

T77. Zoe Trick aka Inverted Angel

Photo 1: From a standing position on the bar, hold the ropes, one hand higher than the other.

NOTE: This trick can also be done with hands at same level. Many students find it a little easier with one hand higher than the other.

Photo 2: Go into a split on the ropes beginning with the leg corresponding to the hand that is lower on the ropes. Inotherwords, that leg begins the split and is on the side of the face and tummy. (front side of the body).

Photos 3 & 4 : From upside down splits, lean toward the side where the arm is lower, bend the leg that is on the back side of the body corresponding to the arm that is up higher…this leg will go in front of the rope.

Photos 5 & 6: The back leg will remain straight and will go behind the rope and the under side of this thigh will lean on the lower hand. With your other hand (hand that is higher up) pull up and face forward.

124

T78. Standing Lay Back Split

Photo 1: Standing on bar, hold ropes with hands about shoulder height bring one leg up as you lay back.

Photo 2: Bend leg you are standing on slightly as you place other foot up above hand on rope as you look back with head.

Photo 3: Straighten standing leg and arch back to create an air split.

T79. Rope Splits aka Snowflake

Photo 1: Standing on bar, hold ropes with hands as high up as you can reach.

Photo 2: Pull body up into a tuck or *Egg (T18)*.

Photo 3: Grab each rope in between your toes. NOTE: Can also be done by placing entire foot or the arch of foot on ropes.

Photo 4: ➡

Straighten out legs as you release into a *Rope Split*.

TA...DA!

T80. Flag on the Ropes aka Iron Cross

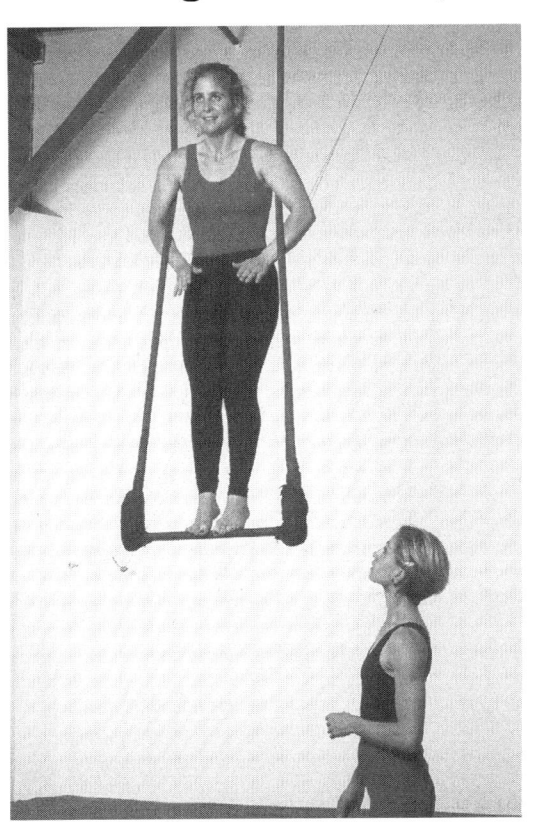

Photo 1: From standing wrap arms from the front to the back of the ropes.

Photo 2: Grab ropes with hands. Try to put the rope in your armpit, and keep your arms as straight as you can.

Photo 3: Take feet off of the bar and tuck.

Photo 4: Extend legs straight behind the bar as you extend arms out to sides.

NOTE: For added support or if this hurts wrists, try rotating wrists until palms face up or forward.

T81. Shoulder Wrap

Photo 1:
Stand on bar facing forward and point one arm straight down and wrap around rope from front to back and grab rope with hand in front.

Photo 2: ➡
Lean body to side with back against rope looking upward as you raise other arm up straight and wrap around the back from the outside to the inside of the rope and grab with hand in front.

NOTE: Whichever side you are doing the Shoulder Wrap on, it is that arm that goes down and the other arm goes up; i.e. in this photo series, the Shoulder Wrap is on the right side, it is the right arm that is down and left arm is up.

Photos 3, 4 & 5: With hands securely holding body, feet are lifted off the bar as you propel yourself around in a circle.

129

T82. 1/2 Angel on the Ropes

Photo 1: Begin with a *Rainbow Split (T71)* (to prep) on ropes then

Photo 2: Wrap one leg around rope starting with rope inside the thigh as you would when wrapping to climb up a Spanish web (page 192) except this is upside down.

Photos 3 & 4: Begin to straighten body and arch back.

Photo 5: Release hand on opposite rope (the rope where leg is NOT wrapped). The other hand is holding rope supporting the body.

Photo 6: Grab free foot with free hand.

Come out of the *1/2 Angel On The Ropes* by reversing the moves and returning to standing position on the bar or going into another trick.

T83. Moscow Angel

Photo 1: Standing on bar, lift arms up to ropes turning hands upside down. Grab ropes with pinky fingers towards sky and thumbs towards ground.

Photo 2: Lean body forward bringing foot to knee.

Photo 3: Arch back and look up as you extend front leg to style.

T84. Wrapped Moscow Angel

Photo 1: Standing on bar, bring leg in front of rope and then wrap behind placing foot on bar.

Photo 2: Do the same with other leg and then lift arms up to ropes turning hands upside down. Grab ropes with pinky fingers towards sky and thumbs towards bar.

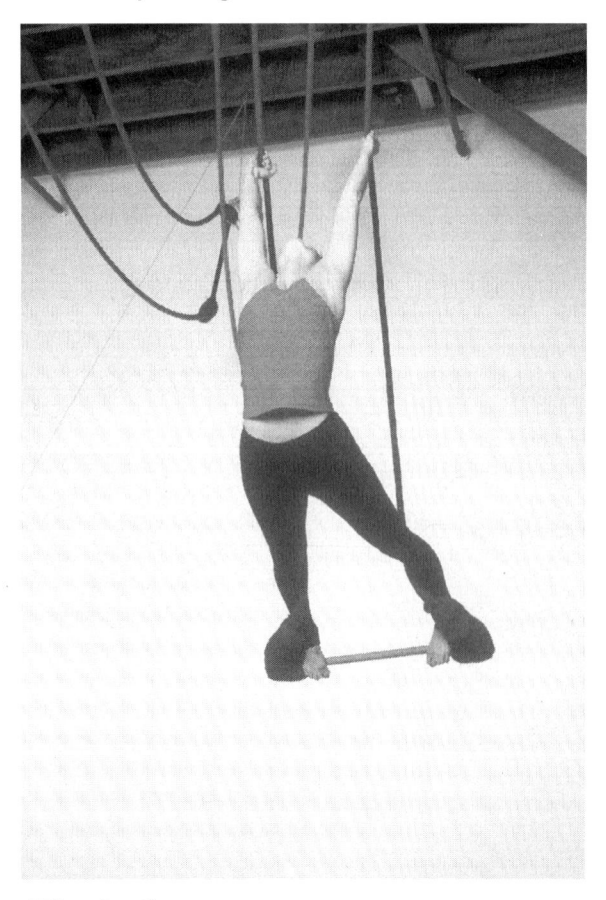

Photo 3: Lean body forward as you arch back and look up.

Photo 4: To come out of trick, you can unwrap one leg at a time or unwrap both legs as demonstrated in photo. Be sure to reverse hand position before unwrapping a leg.

133

T85. Cross

Photo 1: Student begins by sitting on the bar. Place hands low on ropes near the waist.

Photo 2: Keeping arms strong, the student lowers body in front of bar until bar is midway up the back.

Photo 3: Keep the elbows and arms pushing forwards so the shoulders do not go behind the chest and over stretch the shoulders. If the student has shoulders and arms pushed forward correctly, they can then let go of hands and place them out to the side with arms and shoulders still pressing forward to avoid shoulder injury. Note: the bar should be against the meatier part of the mid-back, under the lattisimus dorsi, not as high as the upper back.

Photo 4: To come out, student reaches back to the ropes, slides hands as high as possible so arms are almost straight over head, then slides weight forward and slides hands down ropes until the bar is over the head. Student can then drop down, or do a pullover to *Front Balance*. (T25)

T86. Single Knee Hang

Photos 1 & 2: Single knee hang with foot hooked and unhooked.

Single Knee Hang from Higher Trapeze

Photo 1: Student begins in double knee hang with hips in proper position, pushed forwards, and arms out to side for spotter's ease.

Photo 2: First Position: Have the student straighten one leg keeping knees together encouraging student to secure knees on their own.

Photos 3 & 4: If comfortable, progress to range of motion by bringing leg down to side and around to back, then return to first position **(Photo 2)**.

NOTE TO SPOTTER: When student is doing the trick from a higher trapeze, spotter supports student under shoulders. Be prepared to take student's weight on your shoulder if student falls. The student can then roll over your back, feet first, onto the ground.

T87. Backwards Dismount aka Skin the Cat

Photo 1: Begin in "L" position.

Photos 2 & 3: Descend backwards aiming feet towards ground (front & back views).

Note: If the bar is NOT this low, there are several other ways to dismount. 2 examples include: 1) release one hand and turn until return to original hang position.
2) release both hands and land on feet.

Photo 4: Feet make contact with ground.

Photo 5: Step forward.

Photo 6: Look up.

Photo 7: When securely on ground release hands from bar and style.

Combinations

DISCLAIMER: In doing any aerial trick there is a real chance of injury no matter how "safe" or experienced you are and no matter who is spotting or teaching you. The author, or anyone else whose advice was used in writing this manual, will not be responsible for any injury or misunderstanding resulting from the practice or performance of any feats described in this work-which includes every single page and movement seen in this manual. Purchase or use of this document constitutes agreement of this effect. Furthermore, the author does not use or discuss safety lines in this document. The author advises consulting a professional rigger when it comes to using any safety lines or hanging equipment.

T88. Front Balance Fall to Catcher's Hang (see T26 & T28)

Photos 1 & 2: From the *Front Balance (T26)* spread the legs in a wide straddle and fall forward.

Photo 3: Catch yourself in the *Catcher's Hang (T28)*.

Photo 4: Hold feet with hands to style.

138

T89. Catcher's Roll Up/Angel-Step One
aka Catcher's Hang Rock & Roll Up

Photos 1-6: From *Catcher's Hang (T28)* beat forward, back and up and grab ropes with hands.

Photo 1

Photo 2

Photo 3

Photo 4

Photo 5

Photo 6

Angel - Step Two

Photos 7-9: Pull yourself up and hold up high on ropes: legs are wrapped up in ropes. POSE.

Photo 7

Photo 8

Photo 9

Angel - Step Three

Photos 10-13: One arm at a time comes in front of ropes as hands are placed about waist level on ropes thumbs pointing down.

Photo 10

Photo 11

Photo 12

Photo 13

T90. The Angel

Extend elbows, arch back and look up.

T91. Angel Variations

Photo 1: Foot to knee for style.

Photos 2 & 3: Let go with one hand. As you do this the body will begin to turn.

T92. Angel Dismount

Photo 1: The *Angel* (T90)

Photo 2: From the *Angel (T90)*, contract body backwards.

Photo 3: Arms go up above head high on ropes.

Photo 4: Pull up and release legs from ropes.

Photo 5: Go into tuck position (transition).

Photo 6: Return to bar to a standing position for further rope tricks.

NOTE: You can also dismount by reversing mounting order and going back down into a *Catcher's Hang (T28)*.

T93. Handstand Routine - Rope Leg Wrap- T93-102 is a series

Photo 1:
From the *Rainbow Split (T71)*, wrap both legs around rope starting with rope inside the thigh. NOTE: You wrap legs in this trick just as you would when climbing up a Spanish Web (except here you are upside down).

Prerequisite: *Rainbow Split (T71)* (to prep).

Photos 2 & 3: Front and back views of the *Leg Wrap*.

145

T94. Handstand Routine - Arm Wrap

Photo 1: Wrap arm around rope so that the inside of elbow is against rope.

Photo 2: Continue wrapping arm around rope and grasp rope with hand.

Photo 3 & 4: Wrap second arm around second rope in the same way you wrapped the first arm.

Photo 5: Extend arms out to style.

147

T95. Handstand Routine - The Handstand

T95-102 is photographed partly still and partly spinning. This particular series, like many of the tricks and combinations, can be done either still or spinning.

Photos 1 & 2: Unwrap arms and place hands on bar.

Photos 3 & 4: Press bar out, arch back and look up.

148

Photos 3 & 4: Take one hand off bar and style.

T96. Shoulder Stand- a continuation of the Handstand Routine

Photos 1 & 2: Bend elbows in front of ropes to descend to bar. Keep head in front of bar.

Photo 3: Rest back of neck on bar gently while straightening out arms behind ropes.

Photo 4: Support self using shoulders in the *Shoulder Stand* Style.

T97. Shoulder Stand Slide Down

Photo 1: Begin to contract shoulders and slide body down the ropes.

Photos 2 & 3: Bring arms into your sides as you slide in a controlled downward manner.

T98. Leg Wrap Back Style

Photo:
From the *Shoulder Stand Slide Down (T97)*, release hands and style supporting self with back and wrapped legs.

T99. Shoulder Stand Cradle Dismount

Photo 1: From the *Leg Wrap Back Style (T98)*, or directly from the *Shoulder Stand Slide Down (T97)*, place hands on bar and hold securely.

Photo 2: Release legs. When first learning it is advisable to release one leg at a time. Once student feels more comfortable with this step, s/he can release both legs at the same time, in which case, arms will be providing more support as legs release.

Photo 3: Gently straighten arms as body is lowered down.

Photo 4: Release into a cradle.

T100. Leg Wrap Back Style Variation

Photo 1: From the *Leg Wrap Back Style (T98)* position...You can spin in this position if you like.

Photo 2: Unwrap one leg and bend one knee as you bring arms in to style.

Photo 3: Open arms up to style as spin continues.

Photo 4: Straighten bent knee and release wrapped leg into a bent position which is a *Single Knee Lay Back (T47)* position. Style.

T101. Leg Wrap Cradle Dismount

Photos 1 & 2: From the *Leg Wrap Back Style Variation (T98)...*

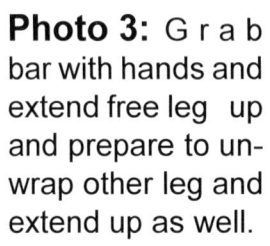

Photo 3: Grab bar with hands and extend free leg up and prepare to unwrap other leg and extend up as well.

Photos 4, 5, & 6: Release into cradle.

T102. Hip - 1/2 Angel Combination aka Gazelle slide to Angel

Photo 1: Do a version of the *Hip Hang* AKA *Single Knee Lay Back (T47)*.

Photo 2: Hold with hand on bar (opposite hand from hip that you are hanging from).

Photo 3: Straighten out leg on side you are hanging from and begin to slide down.

Photo 4: Continue sliding down while circling other leg up then down so that you complete the slide down landing into a ½ Angel (T37).

Photo 5: ½ Angel (T37) foot to knee.

Photo 6: Fully extended ½ Angel (T37).

NOTE: In this ½ Angel, toes are pointed rather than flexed. It is standard to have flexed toes; however, in Aerial Dance, toes are often pointed in these types of tricks. Just be sure you feel secure as potential to slide out of the ½ Angel increases with pointed toes.

Sterling Slide - Part One

Photos 1 & 2:
Prerequisite: Shoulder Stand (T96) front & back views.

Photo 3:
From the *Shoulder Stand (T96)*, release one leg.

Photo 4:
Rotate body to outside of rope while gripping with other leg and shoulder.

Photo 5:
Do a "One Shoulder Stand" supporting self with wrapped leg and one shoulder on bar.

Sterling Slide - Part Two

Photo 6:
Slide downward as you rotate back toward bar while gripping the bar with inside hand and laying hip over bar until in secure pose.

Photo 7:
Release hand and style.

Photo 8:
Dismount by grabbing bar and sliding off.

NOTE: You can dismount out of this trick by simply sliding off or by going into a *Rainbow Split (T23)* dismount.

T104. 1/4 Angel Roll

Prerequisite: *1/4 Angel on the Ropes (T70)*.

Photo 1: When going into the *1/4 Angel (T70)* on the Ropes, kick the bar slightly so that it swings as you go into the *1/4 Angel*.

Photo 2: Grab bar with free foot.

Photo 3: Straighten both legs to create a split, arch and look up.

Photo 4 & 5: Release bottom foot from bar and go into a forward roll.

Photos 6 & 7: Roll forward and raise body up slightly so that your behind lands sitting on the bar.

T105. Dolphin-Rainbow Split Routine

Photo 1: Begin in *Dolphin(T27)* position.

Photos 2 & 3: Fall into *Catcher's Hang (T28)*.

Photo 4 & 5: Hold bar and release legs from *Catcher's Hang (T28)*. Be sure to engage abdominals.

Photo 6 & 7: Using upper body to support weight and being sure to maintain proper shoulder position with abs engaged, bring legs down.

Photo 8 & 9: Pull legs up and into the *Rainbow Split (T23)*.

Dolphin-1/2 Angel Roll

Photos 1 & 2: Begin with *Dolphin (T27)*.

Photo 3: Place one hand on opposite side of bar. NOTE: This is also taught with palm or hand down.

Photo 4: Roll body forward straightening legs against opposite rope.

Photo 5: Release hand from rope, and bend knees as you move into a tuck.

Photo 6: Straighten leg corresponding to same hand on bar to prepare to go into *1/2 Angel (T37)* while resting other knee on bar.

Photo 7: Hook ankle and begin inversion of body.

Photo 8 & 9: Continue inverting body so tummy faces the ground into *1/2 Angel (T37)*.

T107. Spinning

Photos 1 & 2: Prep for spin by leaning body back as hip directs turn to one side of rope. Allow trapeze to gently turn with motion of body. Do the same to other side.

Photos 3 & 4: Repeat prep again to one or both sides leaning back farther and gaining more momentum for spin.

Photos 5, 6 & 7: When you have gained enough momentum with prep from side to side, bring body into tuck and spin.

Photo 8-12: As you unspin and spin again, photographed are some examples of the various styles and positions you can do.

T108. The Montreal

Photo 1: Stand on the bar holding the ropes.

Photos 2 & 3: Wrap legs around ropes from front to back and place feet on bar.

Photos 4 & 5: Move shoulder of one arm in front of rope and extend that arm to style. Move other arm up over head and grab opposite rope with thumb pointing toward ground.

Photo 6: Then bend the extended arm and grab opposite rope above head. Thumbs are pointing towards ground.

Photos 7 & 8: Your arms should now be crossed, and one hand should be on each rope.

Photos 9 & 10: Pull hands towards each other and then apart. This will allow arms to uncross and rope will form an X across your back.

Photo 11: Now the X has moved down your back and the trapeze has turned you around. Bring your hands up high straightening your arms.

161

Photo 12: Bring your arms through the ropes and lean back.

Photos 13 & 14: Once comfortable, let go of arms and relax into pose.

Photo 15, 16 & 17: Hold up high and pull up and out of the trick. Push bar with feet to make it unspin.

Advanced

The following pages contain a sampling of some of the many Advanced tricks you can learn on the trapeze once you have mastered the basics.

DISCLAIMER: In doing any aerial trick there is a real chance of injury no matter how "safe" or experienced you are and no matter who is spotting or teaching you. The author, or anyone else whose advice was used in writing this manual, will not be responsible for any injury or misunderstanding resulting from the practice or performance of any feats described in this work-which includes every single page and movement seen in this manual. Purchase or use of this document constitutes agreement of this effect. Furthermore, the author does not use or discuss safety lines in this document. The author advises consulting a professional rigger when it comes to using any safety lines or hanging equipment.

AT1. Heel Hang

AT2. Back Balance

Photo 1: Student sits on bar, hands low near waist.

Photo 2: Lean backwards bringing legs over head toward a pike position and bar slides to lower back.

Photos 3: Student opens pike keeping bar at lower back and tries to find the correct balance point. (The point varies depending on flexibility and proportions.)

Important — Abs must be engaged at all times in order to balance and to protect the spine. No flopping! If you are not engaging the abdominal muscles, please be aware that you risk injury.

Photo 4: Gently take hands off rope and adjust balance by bringing hands slowly over your head or out to the side depending on balance point. Keep abs tight and balance with the arms not with the body or the abs.

Photos 5, 6 & 7: To come out, hold ropes with both hands, bring legs back over head in a pike, then sit back on the bar.

AT3. Forward Roll aka Front Hip Circle

Photos 1, 2 & 3: From the *Front Balance (T26)* position, beat arms forward and swing body down and around as you begin to tuck.

Photos 4, 5, 6 & 7: Press forearms against bar and keep body tucked as you complete the *Forward Roll*. NOTE: An alternative is to grab back of thighs instead of pressing forearms against the bar.

Double Trap
AKA
Cradle Act

The following pages contain a photo sampling of a few of the many tricks that two can do together on the Trapeze.

DISCLAIMER: In doing any aerial trick there is a real chance of injury no matter how "safe" or experienced you are and no matter who is spotting or teaching you. The author, or anyone else whose advice was used in writing this manual, will not be responsible for any injury or misunderstanding resulting from the practice or performance of any feats described in this work-which includes every single page and movement seen in this manual. Purchase or use of this document constitutes agreement of this effect. Furthermore, the author does not use or discuss safety lines in this document. The author advises consulting a professional rigger when it comes to using any safety lines or hanging equipment.

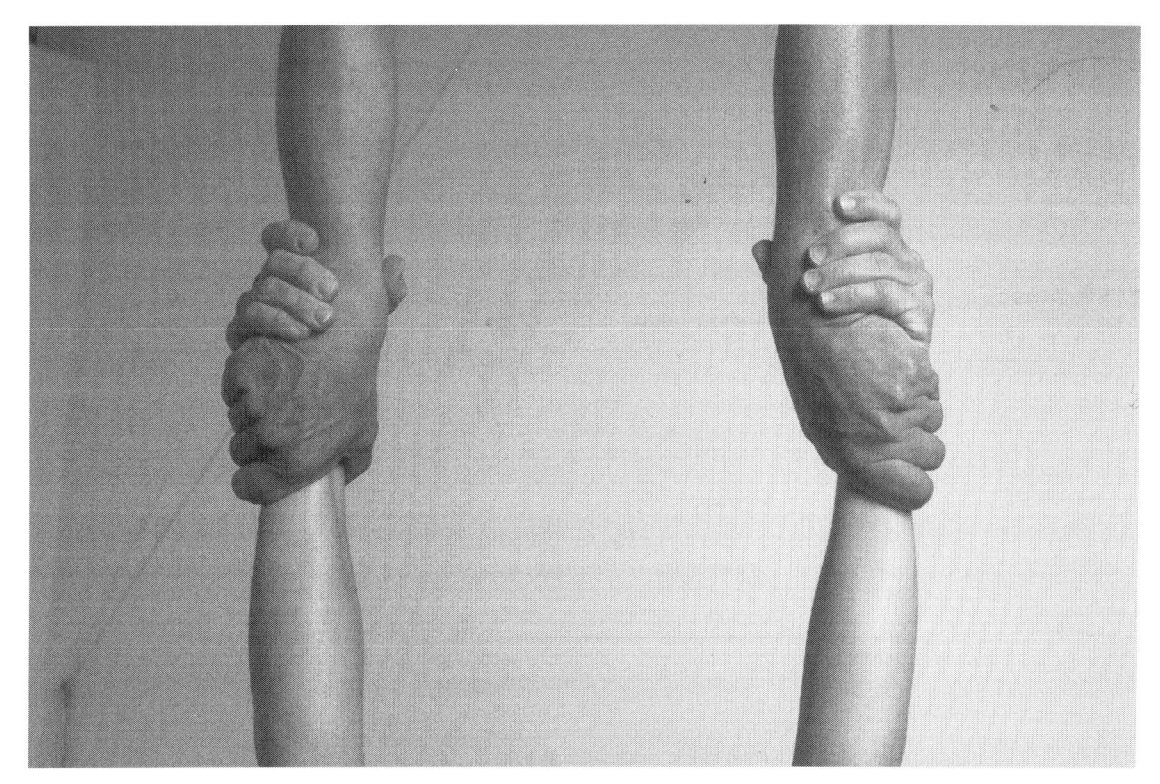

Photo: Hand grip for Doubles work.

DT1. Cindy Alana & Deborah's sequence

Photo 1

Photo 2

Photo 3

Photo 4

169

DT2. Shad & Sara's sequence

Photo 1

Photo 2

Photo 3

Photo 4

DT3. Deborah & Sara's sequence

Photo 1

Photo 2

Photo 3

Photo 4

Photo 5

Photo 6

DT4. Deborah & Shad's sequence

Photo 1

Photo 2

Photo 3

Photo 4

Photo 5

Photo 6

Photo 7

DT5. One Foot Bat Hang

Pose #1

Pose #2

DT6.
Two Foot
Bat Hang

Note: Feet are in 3rd position from Ballet.

DT7. Foot to Foot aka Leg to Leg

Single Point Trapeze

Photos in this section by Don Carson

Susan Murphy, one of the wonderful aerial dancers of today is featured in this section. Susan has a Masters in Modern Dance and is a Certified Movement Analyst from the Laban Institute in NYC.

Susan has created Canopy Studio, a newly founded community arts center located near downtown Athens. In this beautiful space, Susan fosters the teaching and performing of single point trapeze which began with Terry Sendgraff in 1976 in Berkeley, California. Terry created "Motivity" based on the low flying trapeze dance form. In addition to inspiring Susan, Terry Sendgraff has also inspired a whole new generation of aerial dancers all over the country. (Some of the groups include Cathy Gauch of Aircat Aerial Arts in Boulder Colorado, Project Bandaloop based in Oakland, California; Suzanne Kenney of the Pendulum Dance Theatre in Portland, Oregon was introduced to the art by Robert Davidson who also studied with Sendgraff; Anne Bunker of the ORTS Theatre of Dance in Tucson, and Nancy Smith of Frequent Flyers Productions, to name just a few.)

What follows is a small sampling of some of Susan Murphy's work on the Single Point Trapeze. For more information on Canopy go to www.canopystudio.com

DISCLAIMER

In doing any aerial trick there is a real chance of injury no matter how "safe" or experienced you are and no matter who is spotting or teaching you. The author, or anyone else whose advice was used in writing this manual, will not be responsible for any injury or misunderstanding resulting from the practice or performance of any feats described in this work- which includes every single page and movement seen in this manual. Purchase or use of this document constitutes agreement of this effect. Furthermore, the author does not use or discuss safety lines in this document. The author advises consulting a professional rigger when it comes to using any safety lines or hanging equipment.

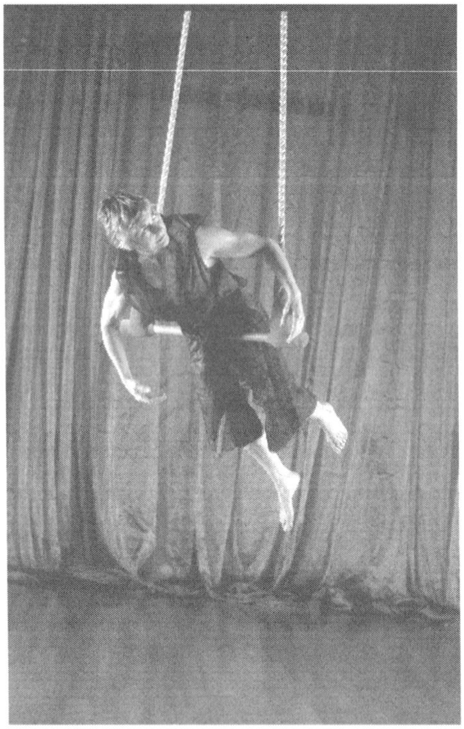

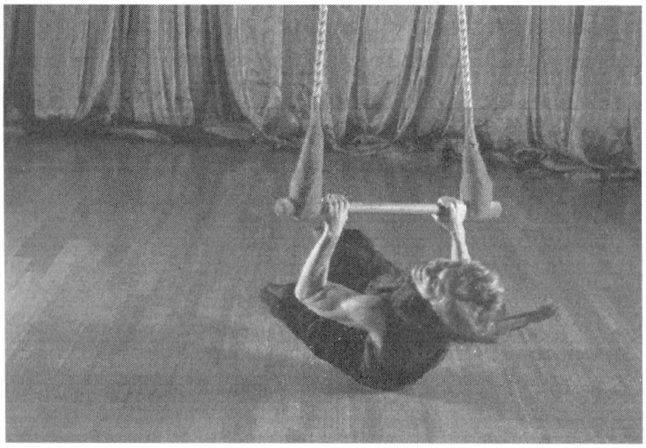

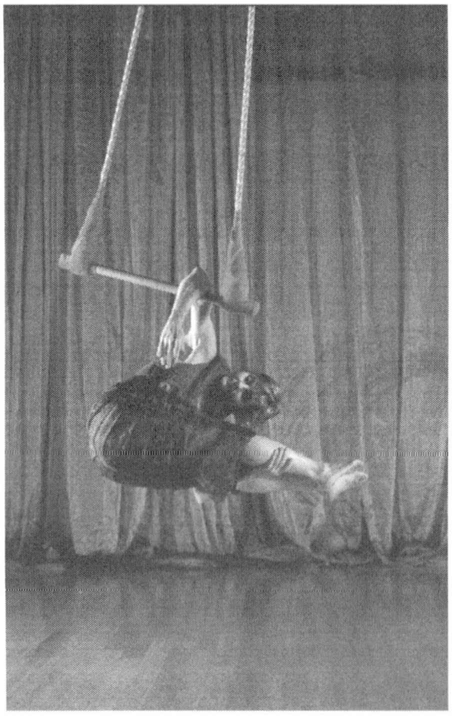

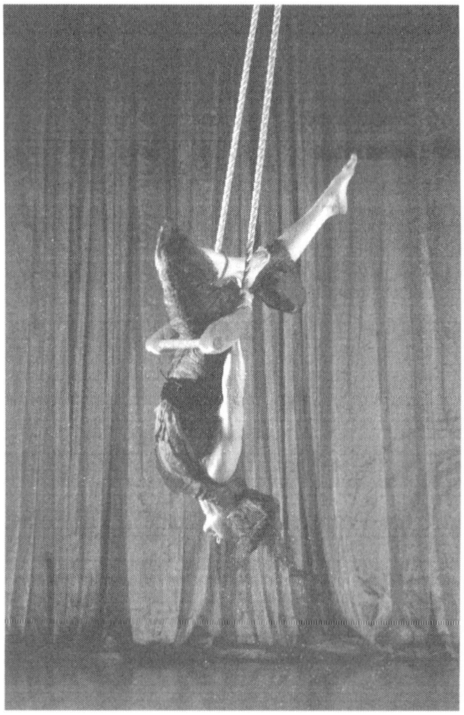

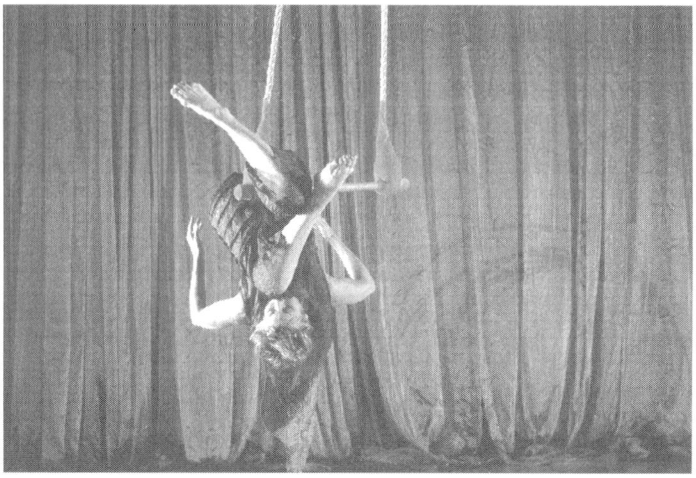

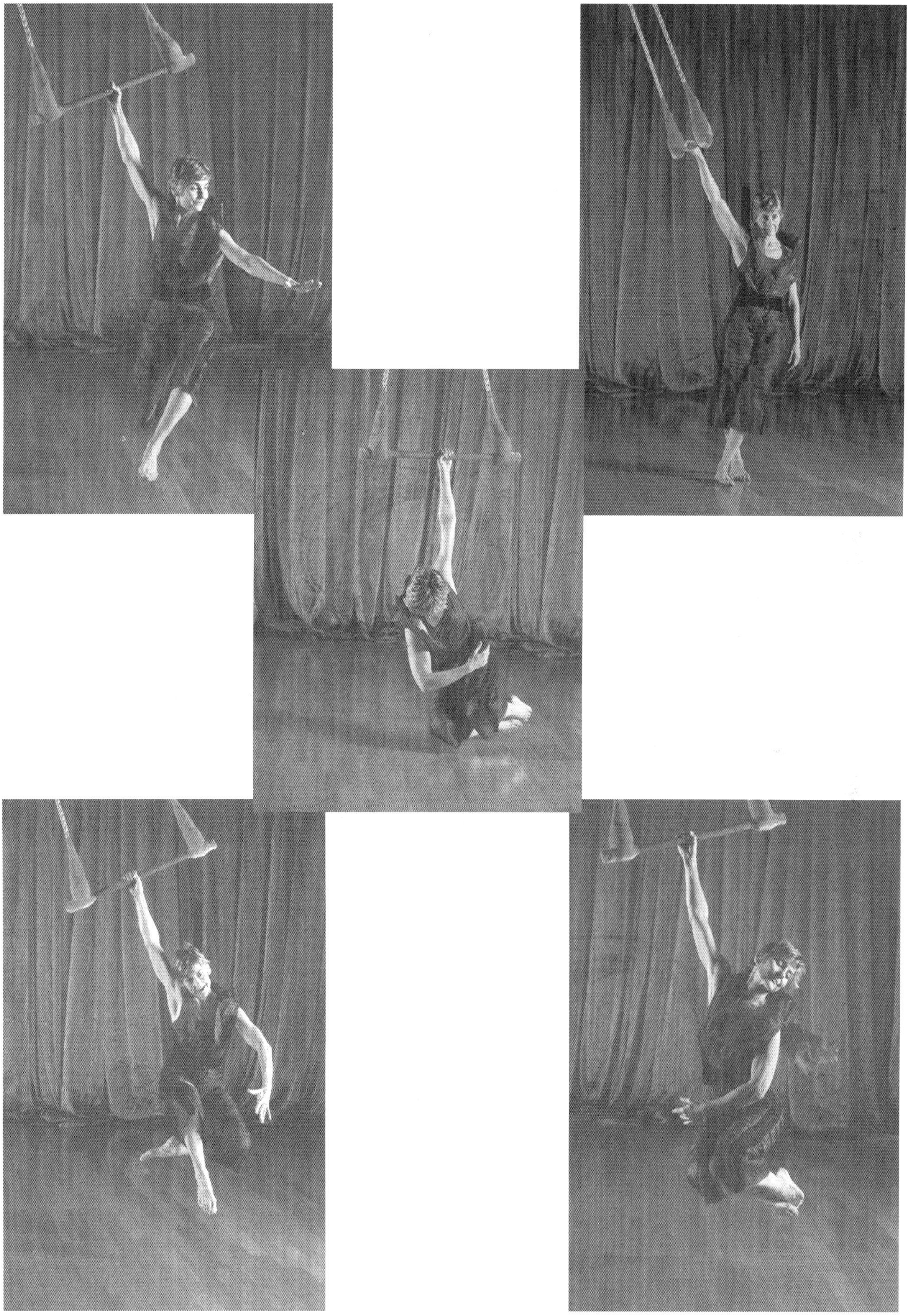

179

Spanish Web

PLEASE NOTE: In some cases, spotters in this manual are positioned a step or two away from the student for the photographic needs of this manual. The position and how to spot is indicated by the photo; however, please note that it is necessary to be CLOSE enough to your student so that you can properly spot and catch them on all occasions. Consequently, when viewing the position of the spotters, be advised that it will be necessary (in most cases) for you to take a step or two CLOSER to your student on the equipment so that you can spot them with greater ease. As a spotter you must have your hands on the student whenever they are doing a new trick.

DISCLAIMER: In doing any aerial trick there is a real chance of injury no matter how "safe" or experienced you are and no matter who is spotting or teaching you. The author, or anyone else whose advice was used in writing this manual, will not be responsible for any injury or misunderstanding resulting from the practice or performance of any feats described in this work-which includes every single page and movement seen in this manual. Purchase or use of this document constitutes agreement of this effect. Furthermore, the author does not use or discuss safety lines in this document. The author advises consulting a professional rigger when it comes to using any safety lines or hanging equipment.

I. Equipment

The Spanish Web is a soft, round, hollow cotton tubing, 2 inches in diameter, with an unbraided cotton/polyester blend rope going through it. One or more hand/foot loops and safety keepers are attached. A swivel can be attached at top of rope for spinning.

It is important to have the web, web covering and hardware attachments checked by a professional at least once every year. Additionally, you should inspect the loops & safety keepers regularly, making sure the loops are tied on securely and there are no tears. Replace the loops and keepers as needed. When sending the web in for repairs, ask that it be inspected thoroughly including the inside materials as well as the covering and all attachments and swivels.

It is very important to keep the Spanish Web dry. If, however, the web gets wet, increase your inspection frequency. If the swivels get wet, dry them with a hair dryer and increase the inspection frequency. You should never pack the Spanish web until it is fully dry. This will help prevent mildew and dry rot.

II. Instructor Notes

1. Setting the web

The standard setter's position is one knee down, the other knee up, and the foot of the bent knee flat on the ground **(Photo 1).** The allows for the climber to 'mount' off the setter's thigh **(Photo 2).** and then place first wrapping leg onto the web **(Photo 3).**

This position is also used for climber to climb first on setter's knee then onto setter's shoulder then onto web at a higher place on the web (often good for performance when you would like there to be less time spent climbing). When I am first teaching students to climb, I will often have them start from the bottom of the web (not mounting off my knee although I am still in the setter's position) and climb from this point up. I place my hand under the foot of the climber to help support them for as long as they need this help **(Photo 3).**

The above mentioned "setter's position" is recommended for spotting. I suggest you NOT lie down flat although this is tempting as it is easier on the neck . I would not spot lying down unless your choreography (or the height of the web) requires you to lie down. Sometimes it is necessary (or may be the spotter's preference) to stand while spotting and this is recommended as needed.

Photo 1

Photo 2

Photo 3

Note to setter/spotter: Hold the web loose (less tension) when person is wrapping leg and tight (more tension) when person is standing.

182

2. Climbing

Photos 1 & 2 demonstrate how to climb by placing unwrapped foot over wrapped foot Climber holds web with both hands, straightens legs while pulling up with hands. Feet are used as "brake" and support. Spotter places hands under climber's feet to help support as needed. There are more photos of how to climb in the first lesson.

Photo 3 demonstrates a rest position where student literally sits on feet while kneeling with foot wrapped.

Photo 1   Photo 2   Photo 3

When two spotters are available and especially with very small kids, a second spotter holds child's body usually around waist. The goal for very small kids is to teach them how to HOLD ON more than anything else; oftentimes their legs are too short to wrap around the web.

Many students have learned other ways to climb up a rope and often prefer to climb that way. Indicate your support for their way of climbing and then make it clear that in Circus class we learn to climb with a leg/foot wrapped, because this is the safest method of climbing. Instructors must keep eyes on the climber's feet because students have a tendency unwrap 1/2 way up the web. Insist that they wrap leg before continuing up, otherwise they must come down.

The exception to all this is for the advanced or very strong student who can climb up the web with no legs, or the advanced student who is learning a more advanced climb (i.e. *Toe Climb-W48*) and/or graceful way of climbing for performance techniques.

3. Swinging

Children (especially very little kids) like to "swing" on the Web. First encourage child to climb a little, then they can swing. Spotter loops Web (where child sits) and holds it while swinging child as seen in the **Photo** below.

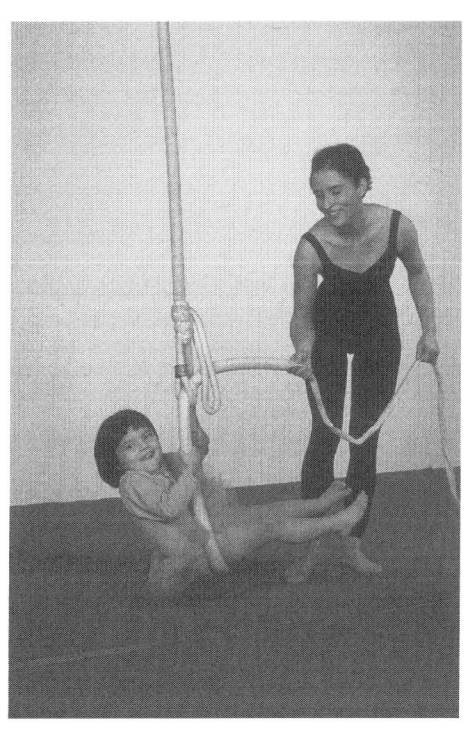

4. Putting hand(s) in the loop

After student has learned to climb all the way up and down the Web, the next step is to teach student how to put their hand in the bottom loop (see W04). THIS IS DONE BEFORE THEY EVER PUT THEIR HAND IN THE TOP LOOP!!!

*Caution** Watch out for students who let go of loop while hand is in...Spotter must be prepared for this!!* Instructor/Spotter shows student how to put hand in loop (under and up W04 photo #1), pull "keeper"-the leather loop-down securely (W04 photos #3, #4, & #5) and instruct student to hold with their hand above the keeper (W04 photo #6).

The next step, whenever possible, is to learn tricks on the bottom loop, then climb to top loop put hand in and begin learning tricks.

Always use proper shoulder position as shown in the trapeze section.

5. Body Balancing

a. Learn to climb with both legs.
b. Switch hands and feet in loops regularly. If right hand is used one week, use left hand the following lesson. Same with feet.

6. Do not slide down the Web unless you are advanced.

This causes painful rope burn. Climb down by reversing steps used to climb up.

7. Climb all the way down

No jumping off Web for beginners.

8. Spinning

Learning how to spin a student on the Spanish Web takes a lot of practice for some people, so don't get frustrated if it is difficult for you to spin someone at first. Be aware that some individuals are more difficult to spin than others.

To spin: Kneel in the setter's position directly under the web. Allow some slack in the rope. If you have both hands on your heart, you spin to the right if student's right hand or foot is in the loop and to the left if student's left hand or foot is in the loop. Another method to determine direction is to visualize a clock on the ceiling and if the right hand or foot is in, you spin clockwise and if the student's left hand or foot is in the loop you spin counterclockwise. Another way to describe proper direction is "opening shoulder and chest."

To avoid and reduce dizziness during and after spinning, it is recommended that the student watch or 'spot' the hand that is in the loop when spinning. Some students prefer to watch or 'spot' the hand that is holding the web; this is personal preference. Furthermore, I recommend you try the technique of nodding/shaking the head after you recover from the spin if you feel dizzy. Rubbing the palms together after coming down is a another method that helps some students with dizziness.

9. Summary of Web Endurance and Strength Tests

1. Before doing any tricks on the high loop, student must be able to climb up and down the Web without tiring and be able to do the trick(s) on the bottom loop.
2. Before doing footwork, student must be able to:
   a. Climb up and down the web using both legs.
   b. Climb up to the top loop, put one hand in the loop, and do a *Cradle, L, Layback, Flag, Handspin.* Student should then switch hands and complete the same routine on the other side before climbing down the web.
3. Complete footwork on both feet from the low and middle loops(if you have middle loop) before moving up to high loop.
2. Before doing Doubles on the web, the student must be able to:
   a. Show considerable endurance and strength.
   b. Have tried some other tricks not part of the standard routine as well as tried to choreograph some of their own stuff.
   c. Experiment on middle double loops first (if you have middle loops) before going to high loops.

10. Rescuing On Web

When a student is in need of rescue on the web, it is important that the rescuer be strong enough to support the student needing to be rescued. Because the student being rescued is probably afraid, upset and tired it is also important for rescuer to speak loudly and clearly when instructing the 'stuck' student.

If a student is stuck on the web, do whatever you can as an instructor to help them get down safely. There are many ways to accomplish this goal. The photo series on the next few pages demonstrates one way to do a hand rescue and one way to do a foot rescue.

NOTE: You can use a ladder to help with a rescue if you are comfortable using it. Also, you can get on someone else's shoulders to help rescue.

Hand Rescue

1. If a second teacher/spotter is available, then that person is called over to either spot the Web or become the rescuer: **Photo 1.**
2. The rescuer climbs up Web and instructs the 'stuck' student to put her feet on rescuer's shoulders while the other spotter spots/sets the web: **Photos 2, 3 & 4.**
3. Next the rescuer instructs the student to sit on rescuer's shoulders for support. (Sometimes, of course, this step is not necessary, but often the student is exhausted by now and finds it easier to take hand out if sitting): **Photo 5.**
4. Rescuer instructs student to take hand out of loop. Rescuer might have to climb up a little with student on their back to enable student to take hand out of loop: **Photo 6.**
5. Rescuer then climbs down with student on them. (Again sometimes student has enough strength to climb down herself): **Photo 7-11 next page.**

Photo 1

Photo 2

Photo 3

Photo 4

Photo 5

Photo 6

Photo 7

Photo 8

Photo 9

Photo 10

Photo 11

Photo 12

Foot Rescue

Photo 1: Student is stuck upside down and needs a "Foot Rescue".

Photo 2: If a second teacher/spotter is available then that person is called over to either spot the Web or become the rescuer. The rescuer climbs up Web and instructs the 'stuck' student to allow herself to be supported on rescuer's back and shoulders and walk up the web with her hands. The rescuer can also use a hand to support student's back. The other spotter spots/sets the web.

Photos 3, 4 & 5: Rescuer continues to climb up with student on her back/shoulder while student continues to walk up the web with her hands.

188

Photo 6:
Next, the student must wrap her free leg to support herself with the rescuer 'spotting' with a hand under the foot for support. Rescuer instructs student to take foot out of loop.

Photos 7, 8, 9, 10 & 11:
Rescuer then climbs down with student on them. (Again sometimes student has enough strength to climb down herself.)

11. Other Notes To Instructors

1. Look in the mirror to help see if hand or foot is in loop properly and securely. This will help provide a better angle to see in addition to looking straight up. Call another person to look if you still cannot see yourself from the angle you are spotting from.
2. After a student is comfortable doing a trick, you may rotate slightly (as opposed to "spinning") during portions of his/her routine. Especially good to prepare for performances.
3. Spotters, I recommend you do additional neck stretches before, during and after you spot the web, since you are constantly looking up to spot.
4. I recommend trying a foot/ankle covering of some sort when doing footwork. Any ankle 'support' (like a neoprine bootie), athletic tape, Ace Bandage, etc... that provides padding/covering of some sort is appropriate.

Photo: Example of the use of mirrors to aid visibility of the student's hand in the loop.

III. Tricks
W01. The First Lesson: Learning to Climb

It takes a lot of strength to climb up a rope, in this case, the "Spanish Web." Before learning to climb, please become familiar with the Web and evaluate your strength by trying the following exercises.

Photo 1: Begin by holding up high on web with both hands using Proper Body Position. Maintain this position while trying the next 2 hangs.

Photo 2: If you feel strong enough to do so, lift up feet and hang so that you can feel your own body weight.

Photo 3: Lift feet off ground into the "Egg" supporting yourself.

Leg Wrap

Photos 1 & 2: Demonstration of Leg Wrap from ground and air: Rope begins between legs, then wraps behind and around the outside of the calf, then across to the inside of the foot.

Photos 3 & 4: Place other foot on top of wrapped foot that is flexed. It is advisable to keep foot flexed **(Photo 4)**, although some prefer to sickle **(Photo 3)** the foot instead. Please be advised that it is harder to climb with a sickled foot.

Climbing with both legs

Photos 1 & 2: Hold with hands as you bend knees up, secure foot grip and pull up with arms as legs straighten and you move up the web.

Examples of various styles of climbing: free leg in front or back as seen in **Photos 3 & 4** and circling free leg in **Photos 5-8.**

193

W02. Leg Layback

Photo 1: *Leg Layback* being done low on web with hands holding the web. Leg is wrapped just as for climbing, arms are extended, head hangs back.

Photo 2: *Leg Layback* with two hands holding web and leg extended for style. The setter can also rotate slowly with student in this position.

W03. Serenity Swing

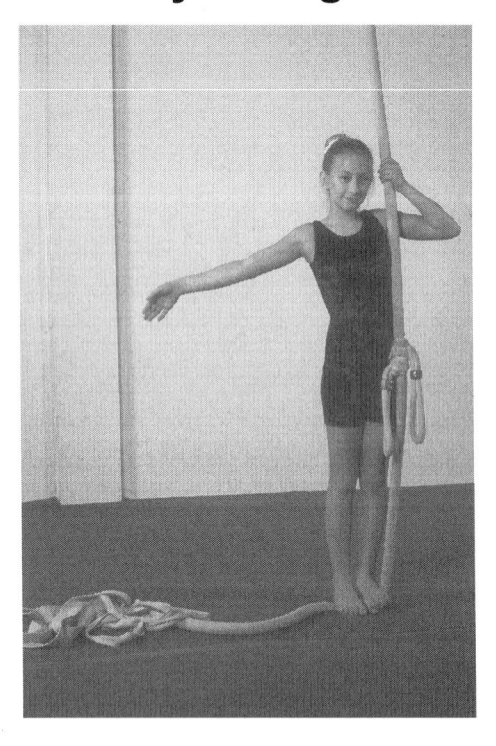

Photo 1: Stand on tight web with both feet while holding web with one hand.

Photos 2 & 3: Keeping body tight and feet strong, lean away from web and sway or swing out and around.

W04. Handloop

Photo 1: Place your hand in the loop with your wrist facing up. Make sure to place the handloop just below the wrist bone instead of closer to the hand so that the hand can grip easily.

Photo 2: Wrap opposite elbow around web for safety.

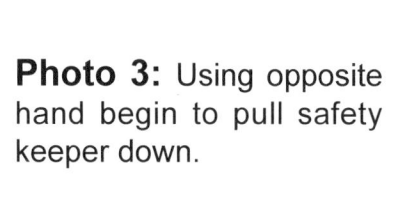

Photo 3: Using opposite hand begin to pull safety keeper down.

NOTE: Similar to the trapeze, it is very important to make sure student has enough strength to progress to the next step. This next step requires that s/he be able to support his/her own body weight climbing up & down the web, with energy to spare, before proceeding to aerial activity on the Spanish Web. Specifically, the student must be able to climb up and down the web using each leg with no rest (touching the ground) in between. For this reason, it is advised to have loops attached at different heights of the web when working with beginners. Additionally, student must learn to body balance and put other hand in the loop.

Photos 4 & 5: Pull safety keeper down tight.

Photo 6: Grasp loop above safety keeper and hold for all tricks.

W05. Loop Layback

Photo 1: Layback being done high on web with one hand in the loop. Leg is wrapped just as for climbing, arms are extended, head hangs back.

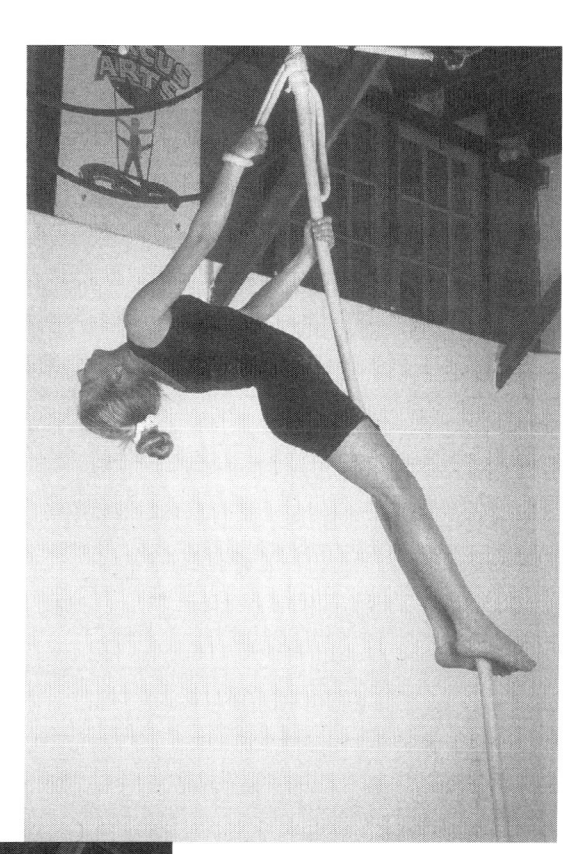

Photo 2: Layback with one hand in the loop and second hand off in style. The setter can also rotate slowly with student in this position.

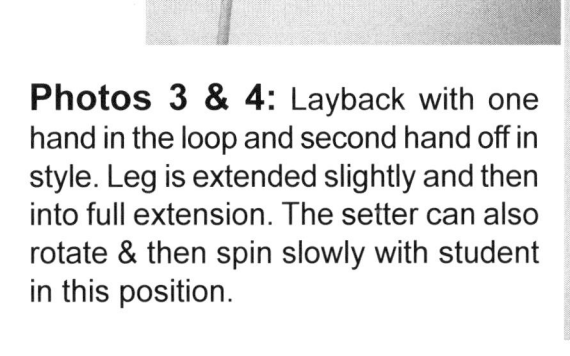

Photos 3 & 4: Layback with one hand in the loop and second hand off in style. Leg is extended slightly and then into full extension. The setter can also rotate & then spin slowly with student in this position.

W06. Handspin

Photo 1: Hand spin position. Spotter instructs student to maintain same shoulder position as on the trapeze to protect shoulders. Each student can choose their own spinning style by experimenting with keeping eyes closed or open and with spotting (watching) the hand in loop or hand on web.

Photo 2:
Rotation: Very little spin and very slow at first. Before accelerating from rotation to spin, spotter checks in with student to see if they want to go any faster.

Photos 3, 4, & 5:
When student is spinning fast, she may take her hand off the web and put it behind her back as spin continues.

Notes: A small arch helps with spin. Watch student's hand in the loop and make sure she is holding on the whole time. Sometimes students will let go of loop while doing a trick if they get tired.

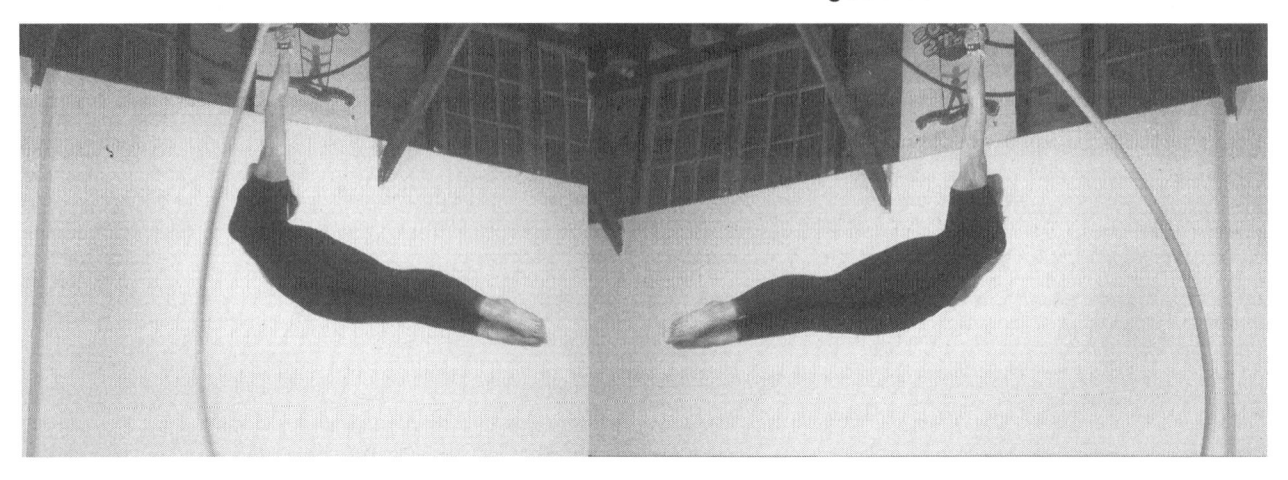

Photos 6 & 7: When student is ready to stop, they can do a "foot-to-knee" for style while reaching out with hand to let spotter put web into their hand.

Photo 8: Spotter instructs student to hold pose until spin comes to a complete stop.

Photo 9 & 10: Graceful way to end hand spin and return leg to web/preparing to wrap.

W07. Cannonball

Prerequisite: *Hand Spin* (W06) with 1 arm.

Photo: Tuck and prepare to spin FAST!

W08. Flag-Out aka Star

Photo 1: Spotter holds web with some tension so student's foot can firmly grip web. Many students like to grip the web in between their big toe and second toe.

Photos 2 & 3: Student can go directly from *Flag* into *Hand Spin* pose.

202

W09. Flo's Flag Wrap

Photo: With hand in loop, wrap leg as if to climb, exent other leg and arm and style.

W10. Cradle aka Bird's Nest

Photo 1: Begin in hand spin pose

Photo 2: Next bring legs up so that ankles rest on rope between upper and lower hands.

Photo 3: Arch back and look up to form cradle.

Photo 4: Same as Cradle in Photo 3 except that legs are straighter as you gently press web away from body with feet to form a slightly different style cradle.

Reminder: learn to do each trick with right & left hand and change sides with each lesson. Whenever possible, learn trick on lower loop first.

W11. The "L"

Photos 1 & 2: From the Cradle position, reverse arch and bring body into a tuck position.

OR

Directly from hand spin position bring legs up and go directly into the "L".

Photos 3 & 4: Bring feet in front of web and straighten legs so that thighs rest on hand.

Photos 5 & 6: Straighten body out so that you are literally doing a sideways "L" on the web.

W12. Layback

Photos 1 & 2: From the "L" position, lean back as you begin to open legs up.

OR Directly from hand spin position bring legs up and go directly into the *Layback*.

Photos 3 & 4: Open legs to split web as you then bend top leg to prepare to put on other side of web

Photo 5: Place top leg on other side of web so that web is in between your thighs.

Photo 6: Scoot body forward so that you are sitting on your hand and lay back as you arch.

W13. Dismount from Layback

Layback (W12)

Photo 1: Wrap a leg to prepare for climb.

Photo 2: Release hand after leg securely on.

Photos 3 & 4: Pull body up.

Note to spotter: When doing lay back on the top loop, be sure to instruct student NOT to "drop" out of the trick which can cause jerking to the shoulders. The way to get out of the trick is to wrap a leg and "ease on down".

W14. Freedman Flag

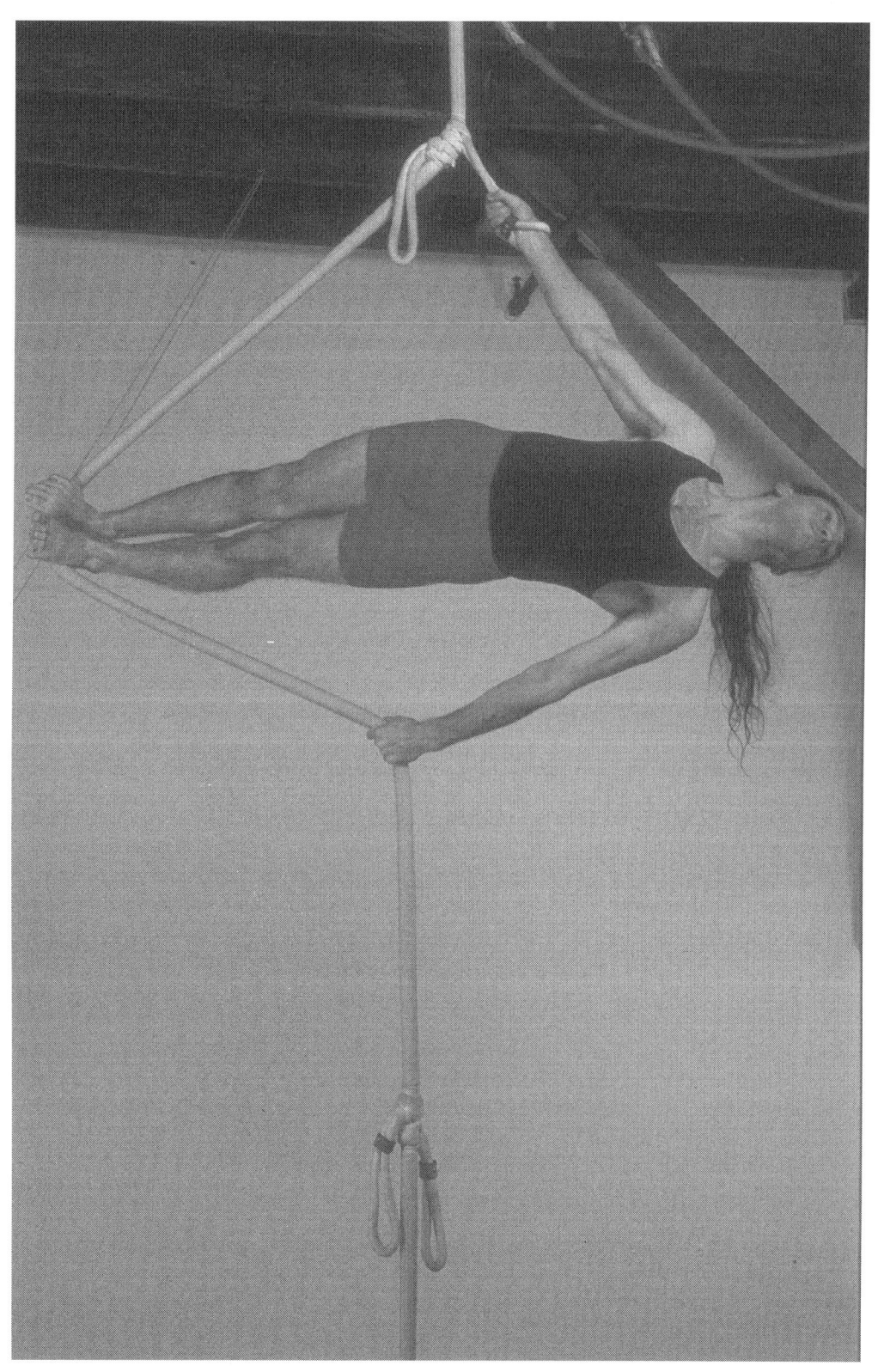

From *Hand Spin (W06)* position, bring legs up and place feet on web about waist level. Straighten legs as you allow hand holding web to gently slide down while still gripping web so that body is parallel to the ground.

W15. Split (with leg wrap)

Photos 1 & 2: With one hand in loop and opposite leg wrapped (in this case wrapped in reverse direction from usual...can be done either way), bring second leg up and place foot on web. Lay back as you extend free arm.

Split (without leg wrap)

Photos 3 & 4: With one hand in loop, make a split on the rope with both legs (spotter must hold tight to help student maintain split in this position).

W16. Rainbow Split

Photos 1 & 2: With one hand in loop and other hand holding the loop, lift body up to form the *Rainbow Split*.

W17. Hand Loop 1/2 Angel

Prerequisite: *Rainbow Split (W16)*.

Photos 1 & 2: From the *Rainbow Split (W16)*, wrap one leg up above hand from front to back. Extend other leg down and hold with free hand.

NOTE: Pay special attention to warming up knees before doing this trick.

W18. Arabesque aka Front Arabesque

Photos 1 & 2: With leg wrapped, position the web across hip of leg that is wrapped. Spotter holds web tight as student leans forward, extends back leg and styles with arms.

Foot can be flexed (**Photo 1)** or "sickled' **(Photo 2).** Please be advised that it is easier to slide with a sickled foot.

NOTE: Try this while standing on the ground first on right then left leg.
Once student is in the air, Spotter must hold web extra tight as s/he is playing a major role in the security of this trick.

W19. Diaper Wrap aka Same Side Wraps

Photo 1: Preparation: Student stands to the side of web that he plans to do trick on. In this example, student will use his left leg to wrap, therefore he stands to the left of the web. After completing the trick from standing on the ground, student can climb up and enter this trick from higher up on rope (rather than from standing), using arms to suspend body then maneuver body to one side of web.

Photo 2: Lift body up to prepare for trick.

Photo 3: Rainbow split : since student is using left leg to wrap, he has the web to the left side of his body to prepare to wrap leg.

Photo 4: Wrap left leg as you would for climbing except upside down.

Photo 5: Bring web around back using right hand.

Photo 6: Bring web in between legs.

Photo 7: Pull web tight in between legs and allow web to drop behind body as you bring legs together. Web should now be secure and hands can be released. Extend arms out to sides. Push hips forward to help lock position.

213

W20. Diaper Stag

Prerequisite: *Diaper Wrap (W19).*

Photo 1: Hold below wrapped foot as you extend free leg down.

Photo 2: Hold below web.

Photo 3: Arch and look up for *Diaper Stag* pose.

W21. Stag Diaper

Prerequisite: *Diaper Wrap (W19)*.

Photo: *Stag Diaper* – Unwrap top foot and bend that same leg (in this case the left leg) at the knee. At the same time, extend the free leg away from body.

W22. Preparation for Footwork

1. Learn to climb up and down web using each leg.
   This is important because when learning footwork, the student must learn to hang from both the right foot and the left foot to body balance. I recommend an ankle/protective foot covering of some kind when learning and practicing footwork. Most of my students wear this protective covering when performing as well. It is easy to slide when climbing with an ankle support on; therefore, the student must learn to climb with either foot so that when the ankle support is on the one foot s/he is capable of climbing using the opposite foot with no problems.

2. The "footwork" test:
   a. Climb up with one leg, put hand in loop and do *Cradle*, *L*, *Lay Back*, *Flag* and *Hand Spin*.
   b. Without climbing down, switch hands in loop and do the same routine with the other hand.
   c. Climb down with other leg.

NOTE: The "footwork test" serves as a skill and an endurance test. If the student can do this and not show fatigue, then s/he is, in most cases, ready to do footwork.

W23. Footwork on the Bottom Loop

Photo 1: Climb to loop (even if you can touch the ground, simulate a climb).

NOTE: Spotter can keep hand under climbing foot to help support the student the first time (as demonstrated in the photos), but before student does footwork from top loop, have spotter hold hand lower, not assisting student at all.

Photos 2 & 3: Learn to put foot in lower loop.

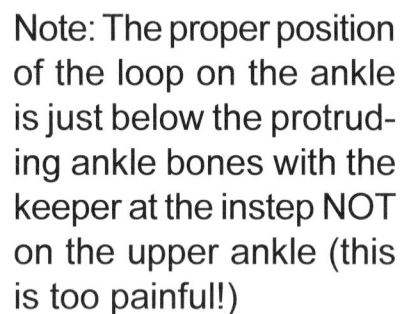

Note: The proper position of the loop on the ankle is just below the protruding ankle bones with the keeper at the instep NOT on the upper ankle (this is too painful!)

Photo 4: Sit on foot.

217

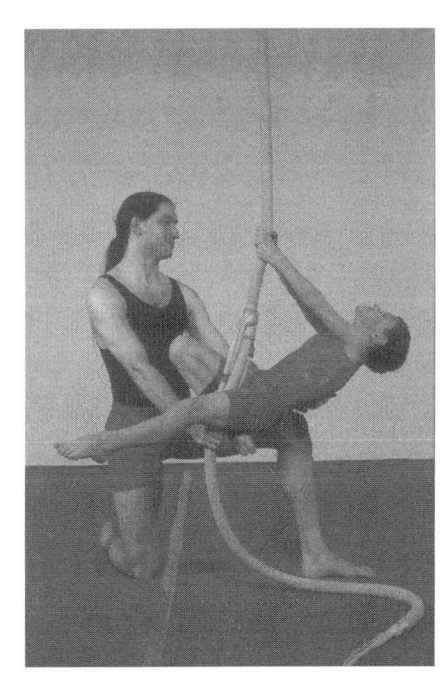

Photos 5 & 6: Lay back with foot wrapped or unwrapped (wrapped leg not pictured here but it is pictured in footwork section on high loop).
a. With 2 hands on **(Photo 5)**
b. With one hand off **(Photo 6)**

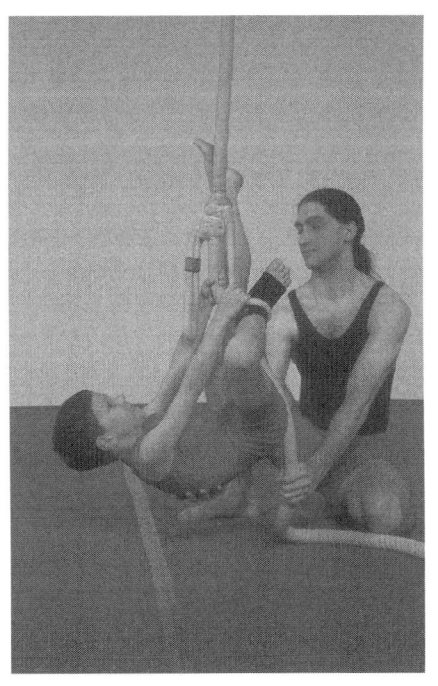

Photos 7 & 8 : Lower body down to hang by one leg or whatever is possible to do from bottom loop. Lower body so that you are extended down to the ground.

NOTE TO SPOTTER: AS BODY LOWERS, INSTRUCT STUDENT TO CHECK AND TIGHTEN KEEPER.

Not Photographed: Climb back up — be able to do this with no help from spotter or from the ground, then repeat with other foot.

REMINDER—*Learn to do each trick with RIGHT AND LEFT FOOT and CHANGE SIDES WITH EACH LESSON. Always wear protective foot covering.*

Footwork-The Basic Routine

Note: If you have a middle loop, do this routine there before going to high loop.

W24. Lay Back

Photos 1 & 2: Sit on foot in loop.

Photo 1: Lay back with foot unwrapped.

Photo 2 : Lay back with foot wrapped.

W25. Descend

Photos 1, 2 & 3: Walk body down rope as legs straighten out.

NOTE TO SPOTTER: AS BODY LOWERS INSTRUCT STUDENT TO CHECK AND TIGHTEN KEEPER.

W26. Upside Down Cross

Photos 1 & 2:
Lower self down.
NOTE: *W37- Wrapped Split* can be used to lower self down and is sometimes preferred with the beginner footwork student as the spotter can assist wrapped leg.

Photos 3 & 4:
Upside Down Cross with back facing web.
NOTE: If the need arises to get self out of this position and/or come back up immediately, please refer to *W35-Climb Back Up*.

W27. Back Pushaway

Prerequisite: Hang down and style in *Upside Down Cross (W26).*

Photo 1 & 2: Hold web under head with both hands and push away.

Photo 3: Walk hands up so back is arched. Drop free leg away from web.

W28. Pushaway

Photo 1: From *Upside Down Cross* (W26) position, turn and face web (if right foot is in the loop then turn to the right. If left foot is in the loop, then turn to the left.)

Photos 2 & 3: *Push Away*: Holding web, push web away straightening arms, drop free leg away from web.

W29. Face the Ground aka Push out or Stand Out

Photo 1: From the *Push-away (W28)*, place foot on web so that legs form a 90 degree angle.

SPOTTER NOW HOLDS WEB TIGHT.

Photo 2: Student straightens leg by pressing against web, takes off hands, presses up so tummy is perpendicular to ground, looks up, arches and styles.

W30. Face the Sky

Photo 1: From *Face the Ground (W29)* position, rotate body up to face sky while carefully rotating the free foot so that it does not slip off web. NOTE: Body rotates towards foot that is in loop. (i.e. If right foot is in loop, turn body to the right.)

Photo 2: Bring face up to knee bending at the waist.

Photo 3: style

Photo 4: Let body relax back down and style.

SPOTTER CONTINUES TO HOLDS WEB TIGHT FOR **Photos 1-4.**

W31. Rope Split

Photos 1 & 2: From *Face The Sky (W30),* bring face up to knee bending at the waist. Reach and hold web with hands while moving foot down the web into split.

Photo 3: Do split holding web with both hands and arching back.

Photo 4: Do split holding web with one hand and arching back while styling with other hand.

W32. Upside Down Flag

Photo 1:
From the *Rope Split (W31)*, grab web about thigh high with hand opposite of foot that is in loop. Release bottom leg out of the split.

Photos 2 & 3:
With hand that corresponds with foot in the loop, grab web at about shoulder height. Turn body into the flag position.

Photo 4:
Extend leg down and style with arm.

W33. Upside Down Flag Rotation

Photos 1-4: Rotate to begin for foot spin
NOTE: rotation here is to the right since the right foot is in the loop.

W34. Foot Spin

Photos 1 & 2: From *Upside Down Flag* (W32) position, begin foot spin. *NOTE: rotation here is to the left (or counterclockwise if you visualize a clock on the ceiling) since the left foot is in the loop. See Instructor Note's page for additional instruction on spinning.*

Photo 3: If desired you can hold free foot with free hand.

Photos 4 & 5: and/or let go of web and hold free foot with both hands.

229

Photo 6 : Come out of foot spin by grabbing web with one then two hands, turning towards web (tummy in), bending elbows to bring body in, and straightening legs up toward sky. This increases the spin-skip this if student is tired or dizzy.

Photo 7: To stop or slow the spin gracefully, do the *Push Away (W28)* by straightening elbows and dropping free leg behind body. Spotter keeps pace with it as the web slows down naturally.

W35. Climb Back Up

Photos 1, 2 & 3: with free leg straight out, pull self up using arms.

Photos 4, & 5 : Or wrap free leg and use it to help you climb up.

NOTE: Recommended stretches after doing footwork include: hip stretch and ankle roll, calf stretch, and hamstring stretch.

Additions to the Basic Footwork Routine

W36. Foot Stand

Photo 1: Stand with foot in loop, foot to knee.

Photo 2: Take one hand off, gently turn around web with elbow bent in lay back position.

Photo 3: Same as **Photo 2** with elbow straight.

W37. Wrapped Split

Photo 1: With one foot in loop and other foot wrapped, slide down web holding with both hands.

Photos 2 & 3: Lay back with one hand off web.

Photo 4: Lay back with both hands off web.

233

W38. Wrapped Split Back Arch

Photo 1: From *Wrapped Split (W37)*, bend knee of the wrapped foot and reach back to grab web with both hands. Hold web under bottom foot and arch back to bring head to foot.

W38. Unwrapped Foot Back Arch

Photo 2: From the *Wrapped Split Back Arch (W38)*, release bottom leg and hold foot with one or two hands.

W39. Web Split

Photo 1: Split to web facing the floor using hands to position self.

Photo 2: Release hands.

Photo 3: Arch back up and style with arms.

235

W40. Knee to Nose

Photo: Hang by one foot, bring other leg straight down bringing knee to nose.

W41. Back Arch

Photo 1: Prerequisite: *Face The Sky (W30)*.

Photo: From *Face the Sky (W30)* let body go down so hands hold web in arch under foot...now foot (leg straight) and hands are on web with body in arched position. Can do a gentle rotation in this position.

W42. 1/2 Angel

Photo 1:
Before completely descending down web hold web with opposite hand from foot that is in loop about waist level.

Photo 2:
With foot in loop and opposite hand holding web, turn body to face ground while extending free leg and arm while arching and looking at extended arm.

Photo 3:
Pull up with arm while turning body over into inverted *1/2 Angel*.

Photo 4:
Switch hands and hold web with same hand as foot that is in the loop.

238

More Body Wraps
W43. Shoulder Wrap aka Cross

Photo 1: With leg wrapped, position the web across hip and around waist so that web begins to lay across the back.

Photo 2: As you lean forward, bring web around back to opposite armpit. Then wrap this arm upward under and then over web holding with hand as wrist lays on web.

Photos 3 & 4: Then take bottom arm and slide hand from front to back in between web and waist. Continue sliding arm through and then grab web with hand, palm facing down and unwrap leg.

NOTE: Spotter can spin you here if you choose. If left arm is up, you rotate or spin toward the left or counterclockwise. If right arm is up, you rotate or spin toward the right or clockwise. I recommend you try this with feet on the ground for the first time.

239

W44. Upside Down Slide aka Same Side Slide

Photo 1: Preparation: Student stands (or if up higher holds self up to side of web using arms) to the side of web that s/he plans to do trick on. In this example student will use his/her left leg to wrap; therefore s/he stands to the left of the web.

Photos 2 & 3: *Rainbow split*: since student is using left leg to wrap, she has the web to the left side of her body to prepare to wrap leg.

Photo 4: Wrap left leg.

Photo 5: While holding onto web with left hand; use right arm to bring the web around back, under right armpit and around arm. Hold web securely with right hand.

240

Photos 6 & 7:
Once secure, drop right leg downward and release left hand off web and style. Begin to slide down the web.

Photos 8 & 9:
Grab free foot with free hand. Continue sliding down the web.

Come out of trick by doing a *Rainbow Split position* (W16) (without hand in loop) then bring feet to ground.

Doubles

The idea is to choreograph your own routines sometimes with one person doing handwork while the other does footwork, both doing handwork, both doing footwork, one can do hand or footwork while the other does body wraps below, or one can be in a high loop while another is in a middle loop! Here are some examples:

W45. Double Flag

Photo 1: Both individuals have right hands in each of 2 loops and do *Flags (W08)* together. To get into this gracefully, first person climbs up and puts hand in loop and hangs as gracefully as possible while second person climbs up, puts hand in loop and puts their hand in second loop and then both individuals go into the flag.

Photos 2 & 3: Once in the *Flag (W08)* position, hold feet and style.

W46. Double Hand Spin Position

Photo 4: Both individuals have right hands in each of 2 loops and do *Hand Spin Poses (W06)* together.

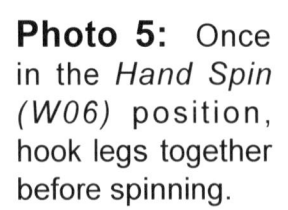

Photo 5: Once in the *Hand Spin (W06)* position, hook legs together before spinning.

W47. Foot & Hand Doubles Combinations

Photos 6 & 7:
One person has hand in loop doing flag while other has foot in loop doing flag... each holds other's hand and foot while rotating.

Photo 8:
One person has hand in loop doing a hand spin pose while other has foot in loop doing a layback.

NOTE: If you are doing routines like these examples, where both individuals are at the same level loop, it is adviseable to do such routines on lower loops first, whenever possible, before progressing to routine on high loops. It is important that the student have the endurance to do Doubles.

Advanced Ways to Climb

W48. Toe Climb

Photo 1: Wedge the web in between the big and next toe as you actually grip the web with those toes and hold with your hands.

Photo 2: Place second foot a foot or two above the first foot using the same technique.

Photos 3 - 6: As you pull up with your arms by climbing hand over hand, you simultaneously 'step' up with your foot as you grip the web with the toes of your top foot and press down while pulling up with the second (bottom) foot. Make sure the size of your steps equals the reach of your hands!

Photos 7-9: As bottom foot 'brings' the web up with the toes, this foot then releases and is placed a couple of feet above the other foot and the same technique is used the entire climb as if you are climbing a ladder.

W49. Straddle Climb

Photo: Climb with legs off web in a straddle and use arms only.

W50. Scissors Climb aka Knee Climb aka Opposite Side Climb

Photo 1: Preparation: Student stands (or if up higher holds self up to side of web using arms) to one side of web to begin. In this example student will begin on her left side; therefore s/he stands to the left of the web.

Photos 2 & 3:
Go into *Rainbow Split* position *(W16)*…web will fall to the left side of body.

Photo 3: "Scissor" the web by bending the knee that is opposite the side that the web has fallen to; in this case the right knee does the "scissoring". Continue to support self with both hands under the 'scissored' knee

Photo 4: Climb above bent knee with one hand.

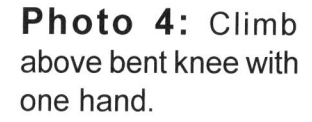

Photo 5: Then the other hand.

NOTE: This climb is also taught with 3 hand reaches for each leg position (as opposed to 2 hand reaches as photographed here).

250

Photo 6: Allow both legs to drop as web falls to other side; in this case the right side of the body.

Photo 7: Repeat with other side by going into *Rainbow Split*...web will fall to the right side of body.

Photo 8 "Scissor" the web by bending the knee that is opposite the side that the web has fallen to; in this case the left knee does the "scissoring". Continue to support self with both hands under the 'scissored' knee.

Photo 9: Climb above bent knee with one hand (as pictured), then the other hand as pictured in **Photo 5**. Continue this sequence.

Combinations

W51. J's Leg Wrap Routine

Photo 1: Begin with *Upside Down Cross* (W26).

Photo 2: Hold web with both hands and extend free leg.

Photo 3: Wrap web under free leg.

Photo 4: Contine to wrap web back over leg.

Photo 5: Release web and style.

Photo 6 & 7: Hold web with corresponding hand of free leg and style. (Same photo different view).

Photo 8: Wrap web high up on thigh and put leg behind you, hold web with both hands, and arch back.

Photo 9: Release one hand and style.

From this position **(Photo 6)** you can also *go into the Wrapped Split Back Arch (W38).*

Photo 10: Begin to lay back and reach for web.

Photo 11: Bend knee of the wrapped foot and reach back to grab web with both hands. Hold web under bottom foot and arch back to bring head to foot to do the *Wrapped Split Back Arch (W38).*

W52. Cindy Alana's Straight Cradle Sequence

Photos 1 & 2: Climb up and put hand in loop.

Photos 3 & 4: From Handspin position, lift feet to rope above lower hand on web. Push body through to the basic *Cradle (W10)* on web.

Photos 5, 6 & 7: Move lower supporting hand along rope alongside the body up to the shoulder area, then turn wrist upward, still holding web, and continue to slide your hold until arm is extended in front of your body. Look out over your extended arm.

NOTE: Spotter: Give slack while extension is in process.

Photos 8 & 9:
You can bend top foot to knee and straighten leg below for variations.

W53. The Split Release

Photo 10: To come out of *Straight Cradle (W52)*, roll body upward towards the free leg and web, extend top leg on web above your body. At the same time, with free hand, place web over same side shoulder.

Photo 11: Once web is tight on shoulder, drop other leg below, splitting rope between legs. Free hand can style above as you do the *Split Release*.

NOTE to Spotter: Pull in slack as the web is placed on shoulder then hold web taut.

Photo 12 & 13: To come out of *Split Release*, release upper leg from web, and bring lower leg up to tuck position.

W54. Lauren's Web Combination aka The Basket

Prerequisite: *Straight Cradle (W52)*.

Photos 1 & 2: From the *Straight Cradle (W52)*, simultaneously rotate your hips and shoulders toward the web as you move the hand with the web in it up and over that same side shoulder so that the web is hooked over that side shoulder. At this point you should be in the *Basket,* holding the web close and in front of the body.. Depending on how far the student allowed his/her hips down past the web in the *Straight Cradle (W52)*, he or she may be actually sitting on the web or they may have the web more underneath the back of their knees (as pictured).

Photos 3 & 4:

To move into the *Air Split (W55)*, put the foot that corresponds to the hand in the loop onto the web in front of you, a foot to 2 feet below the keeper.

W55. The Air Split

Photos 5 & 6: Pull your other leg up and over the web, dropping it in front and extend down.

Rings/ Roman Rings

PLEASE NOTE: In some cases, spotters in this manual are positioned a step or two away from the student for the photographic needs of this manual. The position and how to spot is indicated by the photo; however, please note that it is necessary to be CLOSE enough to your student so that you can properly spot and catch them on all occasions. Consequently, when viewing the position of the spotters, be advised that it will be necessary (in most cases) for you to take a step or two CLOSER to your student on the equipment so that you can spot them with greater ease. As a spotter you must have your hands on the student whenever they are doing a new trick.

DISCLAIMER: In doing any aerial trick there is a real chance of injury no matter how "safe" or experienced you are and no matter who is spotting or teaching you. The author, or anyone else whose advice was used in writing this manual, will not be responsible for any injury or misunderstanding resulting from the practice or performance of any feats described in this work-which includes every single page and movement seen in this manual. Purchase or use of this document constitutes agreement of this effect. Furthermore, the author does not use or discuss safety lines in this document. The author advises consulting a professional rigger when it comes to using any safety lines or hanging equipment.

I. Equipment

Circus Rings vary in types, shapes and sizes. I use either stainless steel or chrome plated steel rings. The bar is approximately ¾ inch-1inch in diameter and 9 ¼ " from inside to inside. You can have 'loops' welded on and attach ¾" Double Esterlon ropes (a polyester double braided rope) or cotton/polyester rope threaded through on either end or you can wrap the rope directly around the ring and splice it together without using a 'loop'. Heavy duty carabiners attached to the top thimbles are used to rig the rings from the hang point. I then cover the double esterlon ropes with a cloth covering. I prefer to use a material commonly called "Trigger" which is a combination polyester and cotton. Wash fabric before covering. It is recommended to check welds and rope splices at least every 2 years. It is important to increase the frequency of your checks if the rings are exposed to high moisture environments or conditions. If your equipment is made of steel, it is strongly recommended that you have it chrome plated to keep the steel from rusting when exposed to moisture. Your perspiration contains moisture and salts, which will attack bare metal and could even cause equipment failure and personal injury. The ropes as well as the splice must be checked regularly by a professional rigger. You, as the performer, are responsible for the upkeep and maintenance of your equipment. therefore, you are responsible for your safety. I recommend you have a professional do these checks with you.

II. Instructor Notes

Please refer to *Trapeze Instructor Notes*. The same principals apply here. The only difference is that you are spotting someone on (2) Rings which can separate at times.

Many of the rope tricks listed in the trapeze section may be done on the rings. Some, not all of the examples are given in this section.

III. Tricks
Rings tricks 01-05 make up The First Lesson.

I recommend that all beginning students start with a basic set of tricks, which I call The First Lesson to become acquainted with being on the rings. Once the student is comfortable with these tricks, the instructor should introduce them to the other tricks in this manual, matching difficulty of the trick to the level of the student's ability. Lesson One contains the beginning steps toward skill progression on the rings.

Photo 1: Stand facing the rings and place hands on rings with thumbs wrapped as always. Kick feet up and tuck and pull bent knees into chest. Pull with arms to bring feet over top of rings. (Note: Some students may need help from spotter to get up).

R01. The Knee Hang

Photo 2: Hook knees securely through rings and keep hands holding onto rings. (Getting up for the first time).

Photo 3: Student lets go with hands and hangs down. (Spotter has hands over student's shins).

Sitting in Rings

Photo 1: Grab ropes with hands to prepare to sit up.

Photo 2: Sit up by pulling self up with arms.

R02. Sitting Lay Back

Photo: From a seated position on the rings, grab the ropes at waist level. Gently lean back until the arms are straight. Arch the back and point the toes.

R03. Standing Up

Photo 1: Place one foot inside of ring while holding up high on ropes.

Photo 2: While pulling up with arms, pull other leg through ring to place on inside. Spotter might need to steady the second ring when student is first learning to stand in rings.

Photo 3: With both feet firmly planted in rings, stand up.

R04. The Cradle aka Bird's Nest with Feet in Rings

Photo 1: Go to knees to prepare to do a cradle.

Photo 2: With hands still on rings and thumbs wrapped, hook ankles in rings.

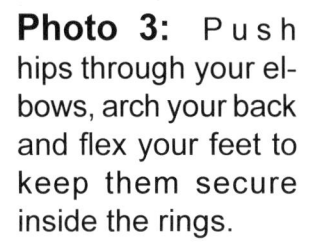

Photo 3: Push hips through your elbows, arch your back and flex your feet to keep them secure inside the rings.

Come out of the cradle by reversing the arch **(Photo 2)** and returning to knees in rings **(Photo 1)** then come down by bringing feet under the rings or simply bring feet straight down.

R05. The Cradle aka Bird's Nest with Feet on Ropes

End of First Lesson

Photo 1: Go to knees to prepare to do a cradle.

Photo 2: With hands still on rings and thumbs wrapped, hook ankles on the ropes just above the rings.

Photo 3: Push hips through your elbows, arch your back and flex your feet to keep them secure against the ropes.

Come out of the cradle by reversing the arch **(Photo 2)** and returning to knees in rings **(Photo 1)** then come down by bringing feet under the rings or simply bring feet straight down.

R06. Standing Lay Back

Photo 1: Prerequisite: Standing.

Photo 2: From a standing position on the rings, grab the ropes at shoulder height or higher, lean gently back, straighten the arms and look back.

R07. One Foot Balance

Photo 1: Prerequisite: Standing.

Photo 2: From standing lift one foot and do foot-to-knee.

R08. One Foot Lay Back

Photo 1: Prerequisite: *One Foot Balance (R07).*

Photo 2: Prerequisite: *Standing Lay Back (R06).*

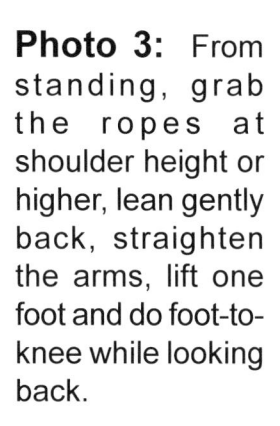

Photo 3: From standing, grab the ropes at shoulder height or higher, lean gently back, straighten the arms, lift one foot and do foot-to-knee while looking back.

R09. Standing Split

Photo: From standing, hold ropes firmly and turn body to one side. Sink into *Split*.

NOTE: Remember to learn the Split on both sides of the body so that you Body Balance.

R10. Standing Straddle

Photo: From standing, hold ropes firmly and face forward. Sink into *Straddle*.

R11. L - Up

Photo 1: Prepare with knees in rings and hands holding ropes.

Photo 2: Straighten the legs into a pike position.

Photo 3 & 4: Shoot legs/hips/torso straight up and over to sitting position.

R12. Rock and Roll Up

Photo 1: Start with knees in rings and hands on ropes or rings.

Photo 2: From the knee hang, swing (beat) your torso back then forward, release hands, and swing down to knee hang position.

Photo 3: Let the momentum lift you up to grab the ropes just above the padding. (Spotter: be sure to watch knees here, especially if you do it with any kind of swing).

Photo 4, 5 & 6: *L up (T09) holding ropes.*

278

R13. 1/2 Angel

Photo 1: Begin in inversion by holding one ring with one hand and putting opposite knee through other ring and hang down.

Photo 2: Invert body so that tummy faces ground. NOTE TO SPOTTER: be sure to spot foot inside of the ring.

Photo 3: Go back into inversion and hold free leg with free hand.

Photo 4: Contract body into ball and begin to spin yourself.

Photo 5: Continue to spin.

Photo 6: Expand body out to ½ angel inversion once again as body turns from the spin motion.

R14. Straight Up & Down

R15. Straight Up & Down Inside Rings

R16. Splits

R17. Dolphin

Photo 1: Hold rings with hands while standing on the ground.

Photos 2, 3 & 4: Pull body upside down and put left leg through left ring and right leg through right ring.

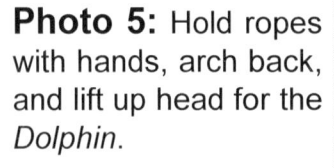

Photo 5: Hold ropes with hands, arch back, and lift up head for the *Dolphin*.

283

R19. Bird (no handed *Angel*)

Photo 1:
Prerequisite: *Angel (R18)*.

Photo 2:
From the *Angel (R18)*, release hands.

R18. Angel

Photo 1:
Prerequisite: *Dolphin (R17)*.

Photo 2:
Position hands a little lower and place feet above hands on ropes.

R21. Forward Roll

Photo 1: Prerequisite: *Hip Hang (R20)*.

Photo 2: From *Hip Hang (R20)*, hold rings with hands.

Photo 3 & 4: Roll forward and come out of the rings.

Photo 5: Return to standing position.

R20. Hip Hang

Photos 1- 4: Prerequisite: First four steps of the *Dophin (R17)*.

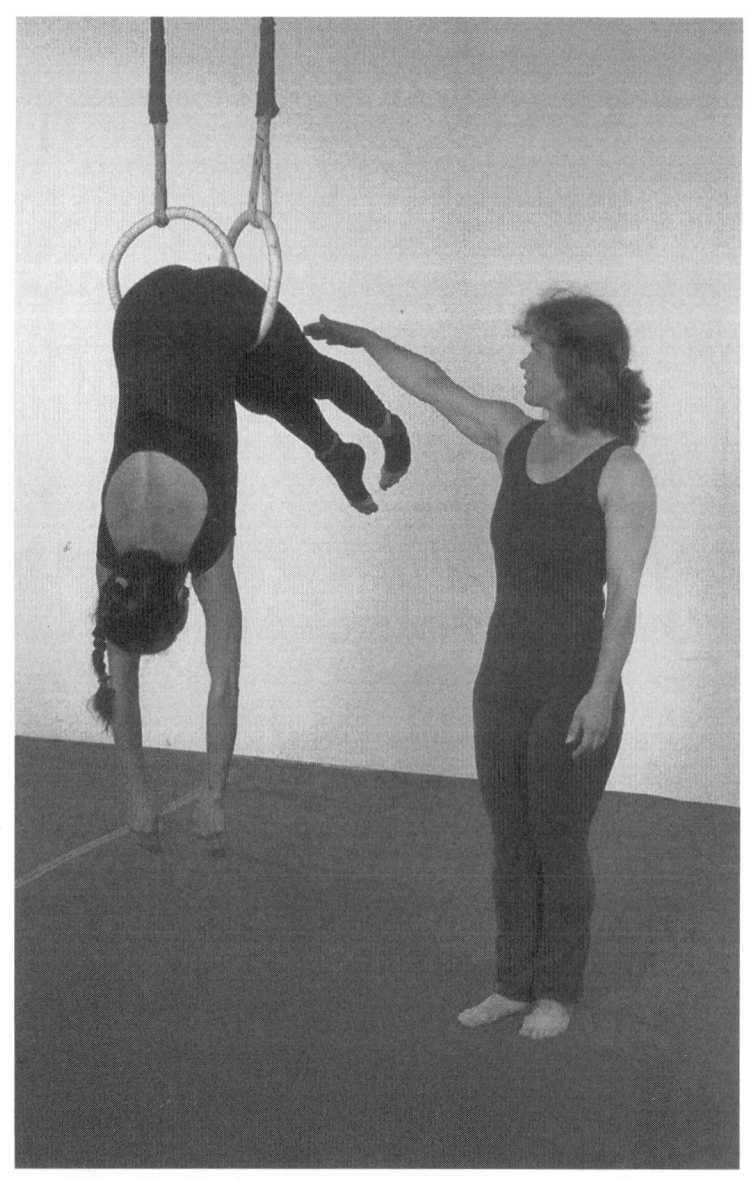

Photo 5: Release hands and hang forward.

R22. Roll Around

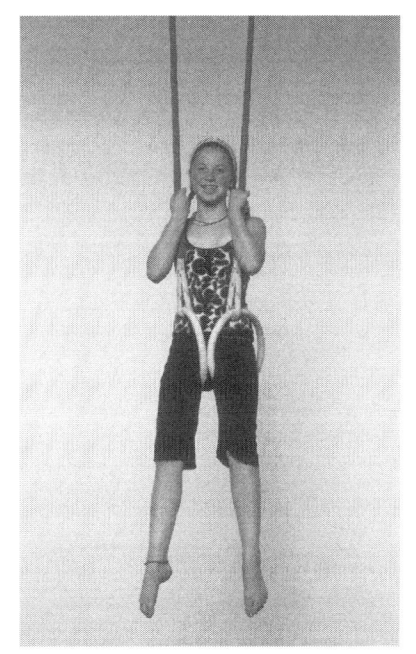

Photo 1: Begin sitting in rings.

Photo 2: Hold ropes low with thumbs in front and begin to lean forward.

Photo 3: Hold rings and roll forward

Photo 4: Regrasp ropes and begin to pull self up.

Photo 5: Pull self up entirely.

Photo 6: Return to sitting position.

NOTE: This is a slow motion/beginners version of another trick that is not photographed called a *Speedy Roll Around* where the hands are always on the ropes and the legs are straight. Here the hands go from the ropes to the rings and back up to the ropes.

R23. Hilary's Sit Cradle

Photo 1: Begin by sitting in the rings.

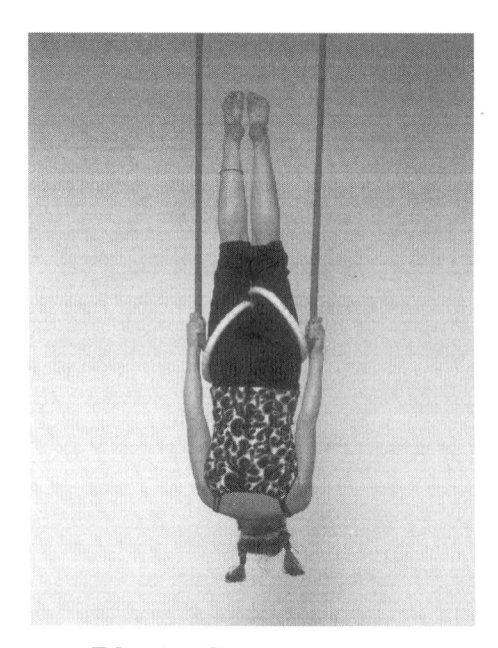

Photo 2: Holding ropes low, do a front roll into a *Straight Up & Down Inside Rings (R15)*.

Photo 3: Hook ankles on ropes.

Photo 4: Bend knees and begin to arch back.

Photo 5: Arch all the way through and SMILE!:)

Photo 6: Do a half angel if you so desire by taking off one foot and extending into pose.

R24. Cradle in one Ring

R25. 1/4 Angel in one Ring

R26. Double Cradles

R27. Cradle on the Ropes

Prerequisite: *Standing (R03)*.

Photo 1: Pull the body up into a tuck where the shins are facing the sky.

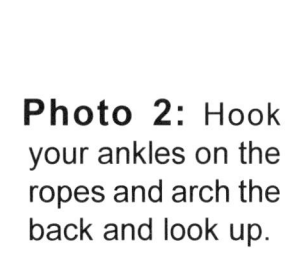

Photo 2: Hook your ankles on the ropes and arch the back and look up.

R28. 1/4 Angel on the Ropes

Prerequisite: *Cradle on the Ropes (R27)*.

Photo 1: From the *Cradle on the Ropes (R27)*, release leg into *1/4 Angel*.

R29. Straight Up & Down on the Ropes

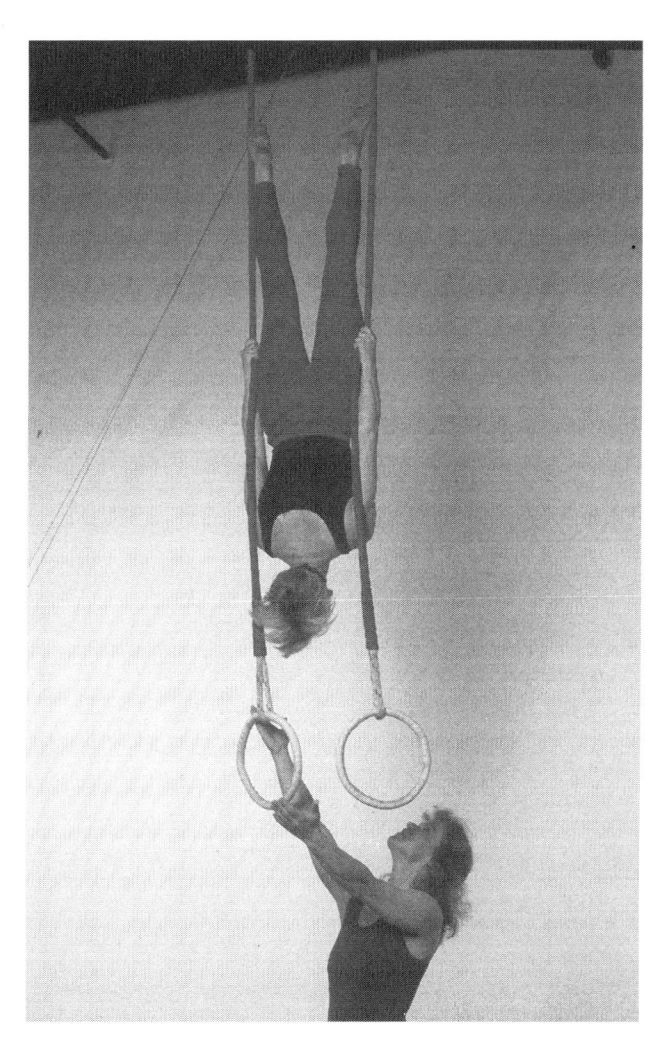

Photo 1: From a standing position in the rings with arms about shoulder height, bring legs up as you would for a *Cradle on the Ropes (R27)*, but instead point feet straight up into the air. To help achieve a balance you can rest feet against ropes.

Photo 2: Once you have achieved balance, make the body straight like a plank. Be sure to look straight ahead so that head is not tilting up OR down but instead pointed straight.

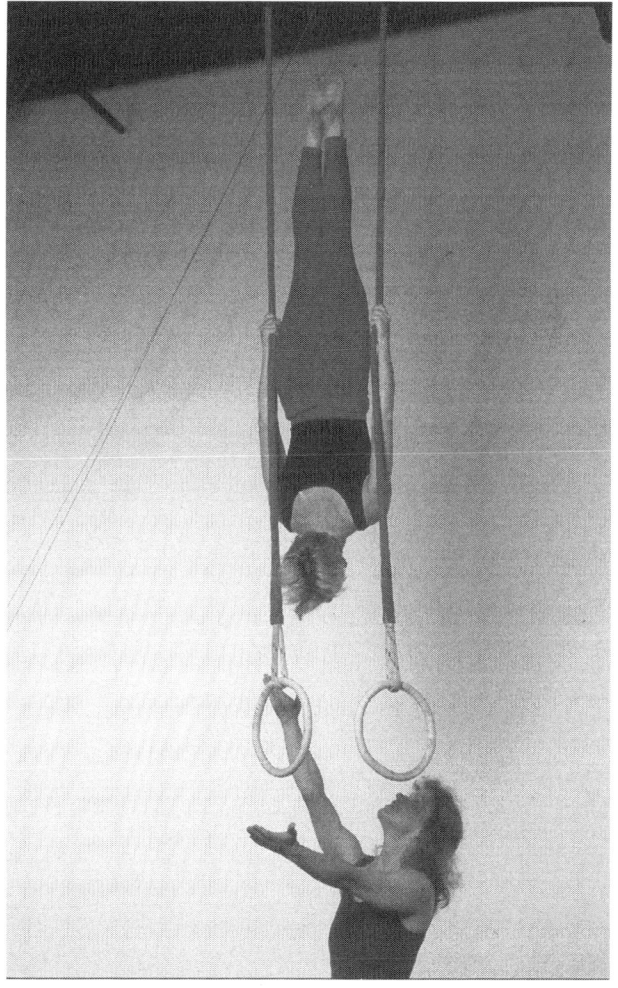

R30. Splits on the Ropes

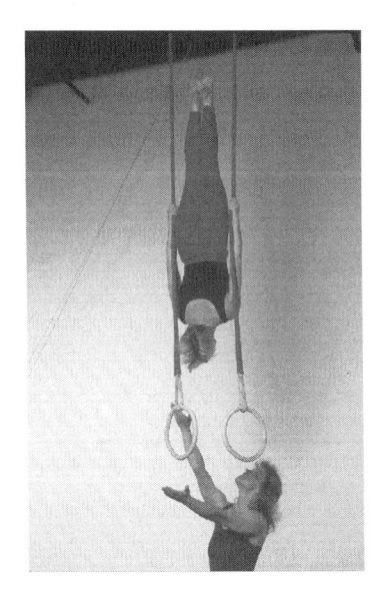

Prerequisite: *Straight Up & Down on the Ropes (R29)*.

Photo: From the *Straight Up & Down (R29)* open legs into a *Split*, gently arching back and tilting head toward back.

Flag on the Ropes-Arm Position

Photos 1 & 2: From standing wrap arms from front to back of the ropes and then hold ropes with hands. The key to this grip is that you put the rope in your armpits.

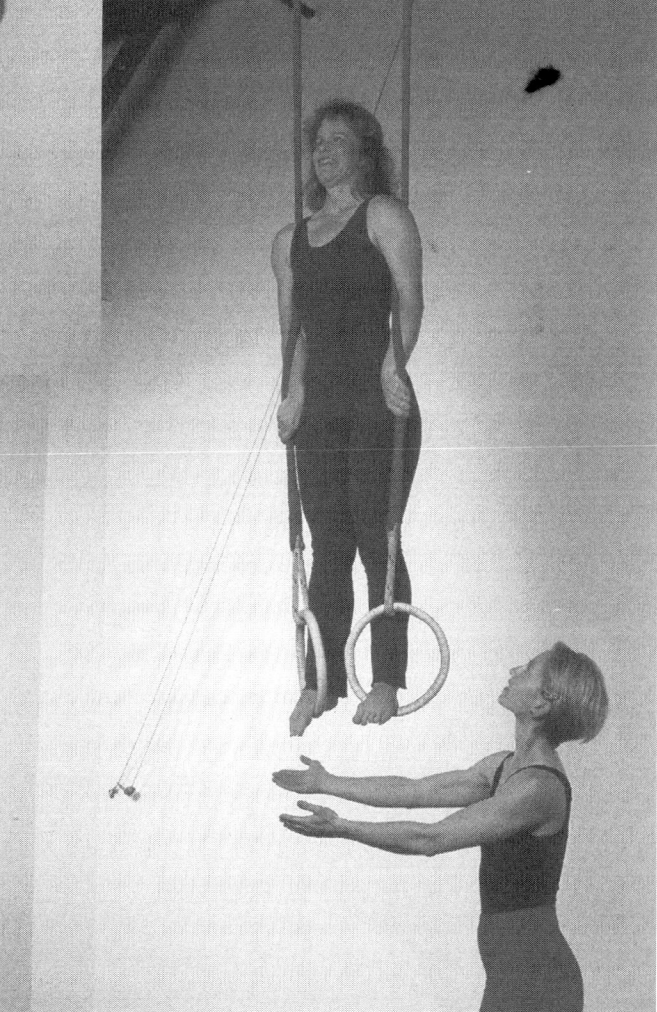

R31. Flag on the Ropes

Photo 1: Prepare arms.

Photo 2: Take your feet out of the rings and extend legs straight as you extend your arms out to your sides. For added support you can turn. For added support or if this hurts wrists, try rotating wrists until palms face up or forward.

Photo 3: Foot to knee.

NOTE: If you look at the "Flag" on the trapeze you will notice the arms are extended wider. This is simply a difference in style and individuality.

R32. Standing Split Spinning

Photo 1-4: Spotter holds student's calves and rotates to prepare for spin.

Photos 5 & 6: Spotter release student's calves and allows her to rotate.

Photos 7 & 8: Bring legs together as you stop.

Tissu/Silk Fabric/ Curtain

The following pages contain a photo sampling of a few of the many tricks that can be done on the Fabric. The foot wraps are explained as these can be done on both the Fabric and the Spanish Web.

DISCLAIMER: In doing any aerial trick there is a real chance of injury no matter how "safe" or experienced you are and no matter who is spotting or teaching you. The author, or anyone else whose advice was used in writing this manual, will not be responsible for any injury or misunderstanding resulting from the practice or performance of any feats described in this work-which includes every single page and movement seen in this manual. Purchase or use of this document constitutes agreement of this effect. Furthermore, the author does not use or discuss safety lines in this document. The author advises consulting a professional rigger when it comes to using any safety lines or hanging equipment.

F1. Figure-8 Foot Lock/Key - Try this sitting on the ground first.

Photo 1: Have one leg wrapped around the rope once as if for a climb, with rope beginning between legs, behind and around the outside of the calf, then across to the inside of the foot.

Photo 2: Take second foot and place toes on the rope above the first foot's wrap. Slide wrapped foot lower to give extra fabric for the next wrap.

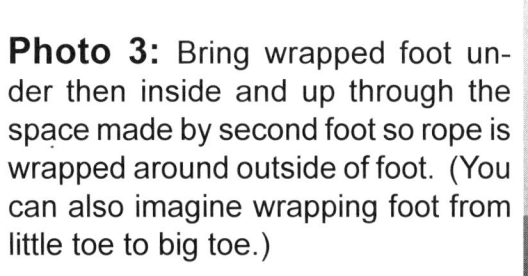

Photo 3: Bring wrapped foot under then inside and up through the space made by second foot so rope is wrapped around outside of foot. (You can also imagine wrapping foot from little toe to big toe.)

Photo 4: Next, step on the wrap you have just made so the weight-bearing end of the fabric is at the instep of the foot.

To come out, hold your weight in your hands, slide wrapped foot back and then down... and the wrap will slide off.

F2. Double Wrap Foot Lock/Key - Try this sitting on the ground first

Photo 1: Have one leg wrapped around the rope once as if for a climb, with rope beginning between legs, behind and around the outside of the calf, then across to the inside of the foot.

Photo 2: Next, add a second wrap in the same direction.

Photo 3: Use free foot to snag fabric behind first leg's knee.

Photo 4: Then lift first foot up so second foot can drop the second wrap down and around the heel of the wrapped foot to create a lock whose "live" end is on the instep of the foot. To get out of the wrap, must slide foot forward to avoid getting tangled.

F3. Splits -

Both feet can be in *Figure 8 (F1) or Double Wrap (F2)*

F4. Arabesque

Foot can be in *Figure 8 (F1) or Double Wrap (F2)*

F5. Frog - from *Same Side Wrap.* See *(W19)* and *Diaper Wrap (W20).*

Lyra/Lyre/Hoop/Cerceaux

The following pages contain a photo sampling of a few of the many tricks that can be done on the Lyra, both solo and with a partner. You can attach hand loops to a Lyra, foot loops, or have no loops.

DISCLAIMER: In doing any aerial trick there is a real chance of injury no matter how "safe" or experienced you are and no matter who is spotting or teaching you. The author, or anyone else whose advice was used in writing this manual, will not be responsible for any injury or misunderstanding resulting from the practice or performance of any feats described in this work-which includes every single page and movement seen in this manual. Purchase or use of this document constitutes agreement of this effect. Furthermore, the author does not use or discuss safety lines in this document. The author advises consulting a professional rigger when it comes to using any safety lines or hanging equipment.

L1. Lyra with Hand Loops - There are several tricks you can do with hands in hand loops on the Lyra, below are two examples

L2. Splits

L3. Double Foot Hang aka Side Ankle Hang

L4. Doubles Single Knee Lay Backs aka Amazon aka Gazelle

L5. Doubles Cradle

Tightwire

The following pages contain photos of the basics – a few of the many tricks that you can do on the tightwire.

DISCLAIMER: In doing any aerial trick there is a real chance of injury no matter how "safe" or experienced you are and no matter who is spotting or teaching you. The author, or anyone else whose advice was used in writing this manual, will not be responsible for any injury or misunderstanding resulting from the practice or performance of any feats described in this work-which includes every single page and movement seen in this manual. Purchase or use of this document constitutes agreement of this effect. Furthermore, the author does not use or discuss safety lines in this document. The author advises consulting a professional rigger when it comes to using any safety lines or hanging equipment.

NOTE: Many camps and circus schools require socks or slippers to avoid toe accidents. Alternate/Advanced foot position involves a slight turnout so the foot can grip the wire. This is for "Dancing on the Wire."

Walking

Spotters:
Tell student to hold onto YOU as needed. Make your ARM/HAND available. No need for YOU to hold onto student unless urgent.

1. Focus eyes on end of rope or wire or at a point in space out in front of you.

2. Breathe from your center... a little below navel.

3. Bend knee(s) to help with balance while learning, use foot not on wire to help center self.

4. Learn to walk forward and backward.

Turning Around

Learn with one foot leading then learn with the other foot leading.

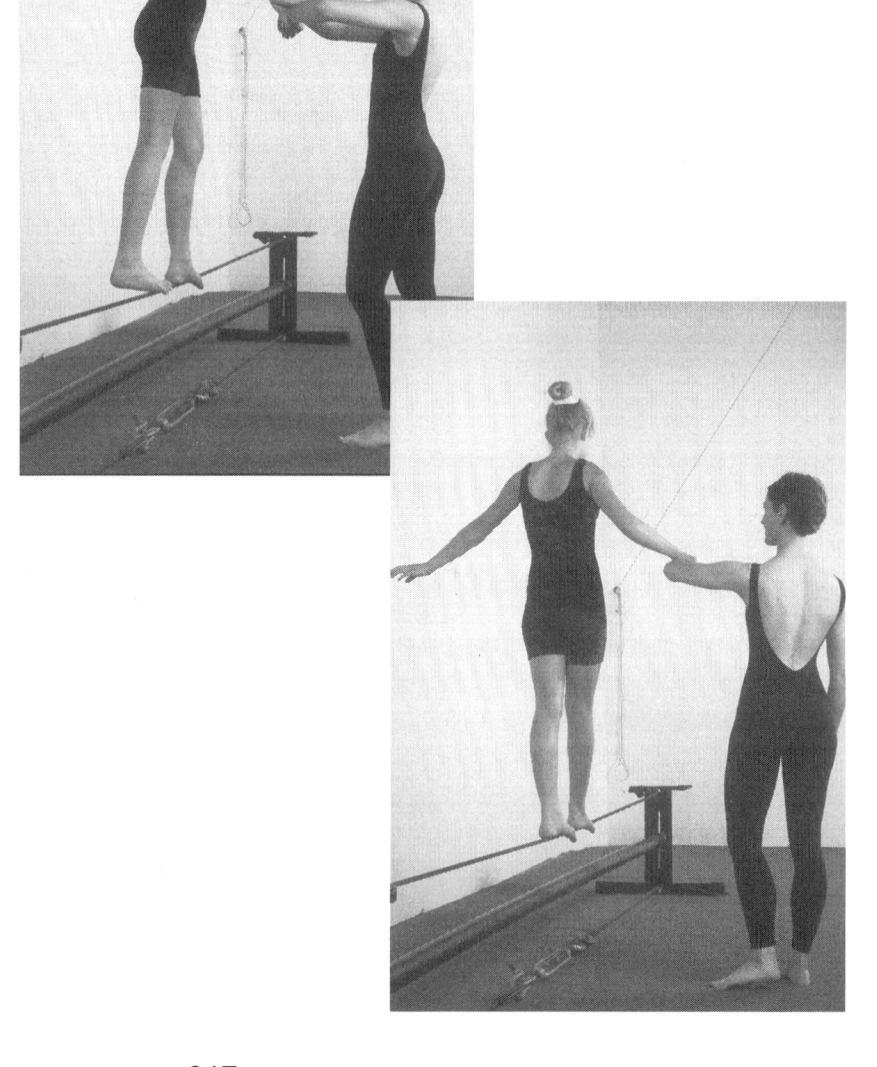

Kneeling

Keeping back straight, bend knees to balance.

Arabesque

Balancing on one foot, lift back leg, extend arms and look up.

Balancing Pole

Walk forward and backward on wire or rope using balancing pole. You can do a lot a 'tricks' with a pole; for example, walking over it, putting it above your head, squatting and sitting to name a few. Make sure to keep abs engaged and shoulder blades pulled down.

TRICK LEVELS

Please bear in mind that assigning levels to tricks is very subjective to each teacher's comfort level spotting, as well as each student's individual level of strength, flexibility and balance.

The Trick Levels below are designed as a guide to help teachers and students keep track of tricks learned and individual progress made.

Circus is a non-competitive activity. It's important to remember that *the only person you can compare yourself to is Yourself..and what you learned your previous lesson.*

Spanish Web

Basic Web
First Lesson: Learning to Climb with Both Legs (W01), 191-193
        Leg Wrap 192
        Climbing 193
Leg Layback (W02), 194
Handloop (W04), 196-197
Handspin and Handspin with hand off (W06) 199-200
Loop Layback (W05) 198
Flag-Out aka Star (W08), 202
Flo's Flag Wrap (W09), 203
Serenity Swing (W03), 195

Intermediate Web
Handwork (W04-W17), 201-211
        Bird's Nest aka Cradle (W10), 204
        L (W11), 205
        Layback (W12) 206
        Dismount from Layback (W13), 207
        Freedman Flag (W14), 208
        Split with Leg Wrap (W15), 209
        Split without Leg Wrap (W15), 209
        Rainbow Split (W16), 210
        Handloop 1/2 Angel (W17), 211
        Cannonball (W07), 201
Front Arabesque aka Arabesque (W18), 212
Diaper Wrap aka Same Side Wraps (W19), 213
Diaper Stag (W20), 214
Stag Diaper (W21), 215
Must first complete endurance Preparation for Footwork (W22), 216
Footwork on the Bottom Loop (W23), 217-218
Shoulder Wrap aka Cross (W43), 239

Advanced Web

Footwork-Basic Routine (W24-W35), 219-231
    Lay Back (W24), 219
    Descend from Lay Back (W25), 220
    Upside Down Cross (W26), 221
    Back Pushaway (W27), 222
    Pushaway (W28), 223
    Face the Ground aka Push Out or Stand Out (W29), 224
    Face the Sky (W30), 225
    Rope Split (W31), 226
    Upside Down Flag (W32), 227
    Upside Down Flag Rotation (W33), 228
    Foot Spin (W34), 229-230
    Climb Back Up (W35), 231

Toe Climb (W48), 245-247
Straddle Climb (W49), 248
Scissors Climb aka Knee Climb aka Opposite Side Climb (W50), 249-251
Upside Down Slide aka Same Side Slide (W44), 240-241
Additions to Basic Footwork Routine (W36-W42), 232-238
    Foot Stand (W36), 232
    Wrapped Split (W37), 233
    Wrapped Split Back Arch (W38), 234
    Web Split (W39), 235
    Knee to Nose (W40), 236
    Back Arch (W41), 237
    1/2 Angel (W42), 238

Combinations (W51-W55), 253-263
    J's Leg Wrap Routine (W51), 253-255
    Cindy Alana's Straight Cradle Sequence (W52), 256-258
    Split Release (W53), 259-260
    Lauren's Web Combination aka Basket (W54), 261-262
    Air Split (W55), 263

Doubles (W45-W47), 242-244
    Double Flag (W45), 242
    Double Hand Spin Position (W46), 243
    Foot & Hand Doubles Combinations (W47), 244

Trapeze

Basic Trapeze
Proper Body Position 45-46
First Lesson: (T01-08), 49-54
    Hang on Bar (T01), 49
    Hook Knees on Bar (T02), 50
    Knee Hang (T02), 50
    Sitting on Bar (T03), 51
    Sitting Lay Back (T04), 52
    Standing Up (T05), 52
    Balancing with Feet (T06), 53
    Squat (T07), 53
    Cradle aka Bird's Nest (T08), 54
L aka Pike (T09), 55
Swing while sitting (T10), 56
Side Lay Back (T11), 57
Leg-Up Side Lay Back variation aka Star (T12), 58
Double Legged Cradle aka Double Legged Birds Nest (T15), 62
1/4 Angel aka One Legged Birds Nest (T16), 62
Standing Lay Back (T17), 62
Squat Routine (T20), 66
Rainbow Split aka Straddle (T23), 70
Sitting Poses (T46), 93
Moscow Angel aka Forward Arch (T83), 132
Mermaid akaTwisting Lay Back aka Fish (T31), 75
Standing X (T65), 113
Rock & Roll Up aka Knee Hang Beat (T29), 73
Standing Up Gracefully (T14), 61

Intermediate Trapeze

Egg (T18), 63 (Strength test for rope work)
Standing Swing (T21), 67-68
Squat to Air Split (T22),
Splits (T13), 59-60
Single Knee Lay Back aka Hip Hang aka Amazon aka Gazelle
    (T47), 94
Ankle Hang (T40), 88
Ankle Hang Dismount (T41), 89
Cradle on the Ropes (T19), 64-65
Double Legged Cradle on the Ropes (T69), 117
1/4 Angel on the Ropes (T70), 118
L-Up aka Rock & Roll (T09), 55
Front Balance with Hands (T25), 71
Dolphin (T27), 71
Catcher's Hang aka Catcher's Lock (T28), 72
1/2 Angel (T37), 84-85
1/2 Angel Inversion aka Angel 3 (T38), 85
Open Angel (T39), 86-87
Fall Back Cradle (T60), 108
Fall Back ¼ Angel (T61), 109
Crescent Moon (T34), 80
Back Walk-Over (T36), 83
Bird Hang (T35), 81-82
Star (T49), 97
Half Bent Star (T50), 97
Bent Star aka Frog Hang (T51), 97
Front Balance (T26), 71
Wrapped Moscow angel (T84), 133
Roll Over aka Foot Flag (T32), 76
Roll-Through (T33), 77-79
Foot Flag aka Roll Over (T32), 76
Scissor Roll (T58), 106
Scissor Roll Around (G59), 107
Scissor Sit aka Cuddle (T57), 105
Dragon Fly (T63), 111

Intermediate Trapeze, con't.

Dragon Catcher aka Mermaid with Ankles Hooked (T64), 111-112
Single Knee Roll Up
    aka One Leg Russian Roll aka One Leg Monkey Roll (T30), 74
Flag (T52), 98-99
Standing Side Lay Back (T66), 114
Bed aka Coffin (T56), 103-104
Monkey Roll aka Forward Roll (T67), 115
One Leg Monkey Roll aka One Leg Russian Roll aka Single
    Knee Roll Up (T30), 74
Single Knee Hang (T86), 135
Monkey Roll onto the Bar aka Double Knee Roll-Up aka
    Russian Roll-Up (T42), 90
Pullover 48
Pullover from standing on the ground (T24), 71
Rainbow Split on the Ropes (T71), 119
Freedman Flag (T75), 122
Rope Splits aka Snowflake (T79), 126-127
Straight Up & Down (T72), 120
Split on the Ropes (T74), 121
Air Split (T44), 92
Single Point Trapeze 176-17
Standing Side Arabesque
Fetal Balance (T54), 101

Intermediate Plus Trapeze

Combinations:
- Front Balance Fall to Catcher's Hang (T88), 138
  - Angel (T90), 142
    - Angel-Step One/ Catcher's Hang Rock & Roll-Up Catcher's Roll-Up (T89), 139
  - Angel-Step Two 140
  - Angel-Step Three 141-142
    - Angel Variations (T91), 143
  - Angel Dismount (T92), 144
- Dolphin-Rainbow Split Routine (T105), 158
- Dolphin-1/2 Angel Roll (T106), 159
- Handstand Routine Rope Leg Wrap (T93), 145
  - Handstand Routine Arm Wrap (T94), 146-147
  - Handstand Routine: Handstand (T95), 148-149
  - Shoulder Stand (T96), 149
  - Leg Wrap Back Style (T98), 150
  - Shoulder Stand Slide Down (T97), 150
  - Shoulder Stand Cradle Dismount (T99), 151
  - Leg Wrap Back Style Variation (T100), 152
  - Leg Wrap Cradle Dismount (T101), 153
- Hip - 1/2 Angel Combination aka Gazelle slide to Angel (T102), 154
- 1/4 Angel Roll (T104), 157
- Montreal (T108), 161-162
- Spinning (T107), 160
- Sterling Slide - Part one (T103), 155
  - Sterling Slide – Part two 156
- Cross (T85), 134
- Fall Back ½ Angel (T62), 110

Arch Up (T55), 102
Double Arm Flag (T53), 100
Sitting Lay Back on the Ropes (T76), 123
Arabesque Monkey Roll (T68), 116
Flag on the Ropes aka Iron Cross (T80), 128
Zoe Trick aka Inverted Angel (T77), 124

Intermediate Plus Trapeze, con't.
One Arm Stand aka Amazon (T43), 91
Sea Horse aka Gazelle Roll-Up (T48), 95-96
Shoulder Wrap (T81), 129
Standing Lay Back Split (T78), 125
1/2 Angel on the Ropes (T82), 130-131

Advanced Trapeze
Inside Out Egg (T73), 120
Advanced section of book: (AT1-AT3), 163-166
Back Balance (AT2), 164-165
Forward Roll aka Front Hip Circle (AT3), 166
Heel Hang (AT1), 164
Double Trap aka Cradle Act 167-175
Hand Grip 168
Cindy Alana & Deborah's sequence (DT1), 169
    Deborah & Sara's sequence (DT3), 171
    Deborah & Shad's sequence (DT4), 172-173
    Foot to Foot aka Leg to Leg (DT7), 175
One Foot Bat Hang (DT5), 174
Shad & Sara's sequence (DT2), 170

INDEX OF TRICKS

Tricks are listed in Alphabetical order and, in some cases, listed as such under appropriate categories. Many tricks have more than one name; I have tried to index each trick under all of the various names that have come to my attention.

Lyra Samples

    Amazon aka Doubles Single Knee Lay Backs aka Gazelle (L4), 313
    Doubles Cradle (L5), 314
    Double Foot Hang aka Side Ankle Hang (L3), 312
    Doubles Single Knee Lay Backs aka Amazon aka Gazelle (L4), 313
    Gazelle aka Amazon aka Doubles Single Knee Lay Backs (L4, 313
    Lyra with Hand Loops (L1), 310
    Side Ankle Hang aka Double Foot Hang (L3), 312
    Splits (L2), 311

Rings

    Angel (R18), 284
    Bird (no handed Angel), (R19), 285
    Birds Nest with feet in rings aka Cradle (R04), 270
    Birds Nest with feet in Ropes aka Cradle (R05), 271
    Cradle aka Birds Nest with feet in Rings (R04), 270
    Cradle aka Birds Nest with feet in Ropes (R05), 271
    Cradle in one Ring (R24), 291
    Cradle on the Ropes (R27), 294
    Dolphin (R17), 283
    Doubles Cradles (R26), 293
    Flag on the Ropes (R31), 298-299
    Forward Roll (R21), 287
    1/2 Angel (R13), 279
    Hilary's Sit Cradle (R23), 289-290
    Hip Hang (R20), 286
    Knee Hang (R01), 267
    L - Up (R11), 277
    One Foot Balance (R07), 272
    One Foot Lay Back (R08), 274
    1/4 Angel in one Ring (R25), 292
    1/4 Angel on the Ropes (R28), 295
    Rock and Roll Up (R12), 278
    Roll Around (R22), 288
    Sitting Lay Back (R02), 268
    Splits (R16), 282
    Splits on the Ropes (R30), 297
    Standing Lay Back (R06), 272
    Standing Split (R09), 275
    Standing Split Spinning (R32), 300
    Standing Straddle (R10), 276
    Standing Up (R03), 269
    Straight Up & Down (R14), 280

Straight Up & Down Inside Rings (R15), 281
Straight Up & Down on the Ropes (R29), 296

Spanish Web
    Additions to Basic Footwork Routine (W36-W42), 232-238
        Back Arch (W41), 237
        Foot Stand (W36), 232
        1/2 Angel (W42), 238
        Knee to Nose (W40), 236
        Web Split (W39), 235
        Wrapped Split (W37), 233
        Wrapped Split Back Arch (W38), 234
    Arabesque aka Front Arabesque (W18), 212
    Combinations (W51-W55), 253-263
        Air Split (W55), 263
        Basket aka Lauren's Web Combination (W54), 261-262
        Cindy Alana's Straight Cradle Sequence (W52), 256-258
        J's Leg Wrap Routine (W51), 253-255
        Lauren's Web Combination aka Basket (W54), 261-262
        Split Release (W53), 259-260
    Cross aka Shoulder Wrap (W43), 239
    Diaper Stag (W20), 214
    Diaper Wrap aka Same Side Wraps (W19), 213
    Doubles (W45-W47), 242-244
        Double Flag (W45), 242
        Double Hand Spin Position (W46), 243
        Foot & Hand Doubles Combinations (W47), 244
    First Lesson: Learning to Climb (W01), 191-193
        Climbing 193
        Hanging 191
        Leg Wrap 192
    Footwork-Basic Routine (W24-W35), 219-231
        Back Pushaway (W27), 222
        Climb Back Up (W35), 231
        Descend from Lay Back (W25), 220
        Face the Ground aka Push Out or Stand Out (W29), 224
        Face the Sky (W30), 225
        Foot Spin (W34), 229-230
        Lay Back (W24), 219
        Pushaway (W28), 223
        Push Out or Stand Out aka Face the Ground (W29), 224
        Rope Split (W31), 226
        Upside Down Cross (W26), 221
        Upside Down Flag (W32), 227

Upside Down Flag Rotation (W33), 228
Footwork on the Bottom Loop (W23), 217-218
Front Arabesque aka Arabesque (W18), 212

Handwork (W04-W17), 196-211
    Bird's Nest aka Cradle (W10), 204
    Cannonball (W07), 201
    Cradle aka Bird's Nest (W10), 204
    Freedman Flag (W14), 208
    Dismount fromLayback (W13), 207
    Flag-Out aka Star (W08), 202
    Flo's Flag Wrap (W09), 203
    Handloop (W04), 196-197
    Handloop 1/2 Angel (W17), 211
    Handspin, (W06) 199-200
    Layback (W12) 206
    Loop Layback (W05) 198
    L (W11), 205
    Rainbow Split (W16), 210
    Split with Leg Wrap (W15), 209
    Split without Let Wrap (W15), 209
    Star aka Flag-Out (W08), 202
Knee Climb aka Opposite Side Climb aka Scissors Climb (W50), 249-251
Leg Layback (W02), 194
Opposite Side Climb aka Scissors Climb aka Knee Climb (W50), 249-251
Preparation for Footwork (W22), 216
Rescues 186-190
Same Side Slide aka Upside Down Slide (W44), 240-241
Same Side Wraps aka Diaper Wrap (W19), 213
Scissors Climb aka Knee Climb aka Opposite Side Climb (W50), 249-251
Stag Diaper (W21), 215
Serenity Swing (W03), 195
Shoulder Wrap aka Cross (W43), 239
Straddle Climb (W49), 248
Toe Climb (W48), 245-247
Upside Down Slide aka Same Side Slide (W44), 240-241

Tissu Samples
    Arabesque (F4), 307
    Double Wrap Foot Lock/Key (F2), 304-305
    Figure-8 Foot Lock/Key (F1), 302-303
    Frog (F5), 308
    Splits (F3), 306

Tightwire Samples
- Arabesque 318
- Balancing Pole 319
- Walking, 316
- Kneeling 318
- Turning Around 317

Trapeze
- Advanced (AT1-AT3), 163-166
  - Back Balance (AT2), 164-165
  - Forward Roll aka Front Hip Circle (AT3), 166
  - Front Hip Circle aka Forward Roll (AT3), 166
  - Heel Hang (AT1), 164
- Air Split (T44), 92
- Amazon aka Single Knee Lay Back aka Hip Hang aka Gazelle (T47), 94
- Amazon aka One Arm Stand (T43), 91
- Angel 3 aka ½ Angel Inversion (T38), 85
- Ankle Hang (T40), 88
- Ankle Hang Dismount (T41), 89
- Arabesque Monkey Roll (T68), 116
- Arch Up (T55), 102
- Back Walk-Over (T36), 83
- Backwards Dismount aka Skin the Cat (T87), 136
- Beat 47
- Bed aka Coffin (T56), 103-104
- Bent Star aka Frog Hang (T51), 97
- Bird Hang (T35), 81-82
- Catcher's Hang aka Catcher's Lock (T28), 72
- Catcher's Lock aka Catcher's Hang (T28), 72
- Coffin aka Bed (T56), 103-104
- Combinations (T88-T107), 137-162
  - Angel (T90), 142
  - Angel Dismount (T92), 144
  - Angel-Step One/ Catcher's Hang Rock & Roll-Up Catcher's Roll-Up (T89), 139
    - Angel-Step Two 140
    - Angel-Step Three 141
  - Angel Variations (T91), 143
  - Catcher's Roll-Up aka Angel-Step One/ Catcher's Hang Rock & Roll-Up (T89), 139
  - Dolphin-1/2 Angel Roll (T106), 159
  - Dolphin-Rainbow Split Routine (T105), 158
  - Front Balance Fall to Catcher's Hang (T88), 138

  Gazelle slide to Angel aka Hip - 1/2 Angel Combination (T102), 154
  Handstand Routine Arm Wrap (T94), 146-147
  Handstand Routine: Handstand (T95), 148-149
  Handstand Routine Rope Leg Wrap (T93), 145
  Hip - 1/2 Angel Combination aka Gazelle slide to Angel (T102), 154
  Leg Wrap Back Style (T98), 150
  Leg Wrap Back Style Variation (T100), 152
  Leg Wrap Cradle Dismount (T101), 153
  Montreal (T108), 161-162
  1/4 Angel Roll (T104), 157
  Shoulder Stand (T96), 149
  Shoulder Stand Cradle Dismount (T99), 151
  Shoulder Stand Slide Down (T97), 150
  Spinning (T107), 160
  Sterling Slide - Part one (T103), 155
    Sterling Slide – Part two 156
Cradle on the Ropes (T19), 64-65
Crescent Moon (T34), 80
Cross (T85), 134
Cuddle aka Scissor Sit (T57), 105
Dolphin (T27), 71
Double Arm Flag (T53), 100
Double Knee Roll-Up aka Monkey Roll onto the Bar aka Russian Roll-Up (T42), 90
Double Legged Birds Nest aka Double Legged Cradle (T15), 62
Double Legged Cradle aka Double Legged Birds Nest (T15), 62
Double Legged Cradle on the Ropes (T69), 117
Double Trap aka Cradle Act 167-175
  Cindy Alana & Deborah's sequence (DT1), 169
  Deborah & Sara's sequence (DT3), 171
  Deborah & Shad's sequence (DT4), 172-173
  Foot to Foot aka Leg to Leg (DT7), 175
  Hand Grip 168
  One Foot Bat Hang (DT5), 174
  Shad & Sara's sequence (DT2), 170
Dragon Fly (T63), 111
Dragon Catcher aka Mermaid with Ankles Hooked (T64) 111-112
Egg (T18), 63
Fall Back Cradle (T60), 108
Fall Back ½ Angel (T61), 110
Fall Back ¼ Angel (T61), 109
Fetal Balance (T54), 101

First Lesson: (T01-08), 49-54
- Balancing with Feet (T06), 53
- Bird's Nest aka Cradle (T08), 54
- Hang on Bar (T01), 49
- Hook Knees on Bar (T02), 50
- Knee Hang (T02), 50
- Sitting Lay Back (T04), 52
- Sitting on Bar (T03), 51
- Squat (T07), 53
- Cradle aka Bird's Nest (T08), 54
- Standing Up (T05), 52

Fish aka Mermaid akaTwisting Lay Back (T31), 75
Flag (T52), 98-99
Flag on the Ropes aka Iron Cross (T80), 128
Foot Flag aka Roll Over (T32), 76
Forward Roll aka Monkey Roll (T67), 115
Freedman Flag (T75), 122
Frog Hang aka Bent Star (T51), 97
Front Balance (T26), 71
Front Balance with Hands (T25), 71
Gazelle aka Amazon aka Single Knee Lay Back aka Hip Hang aka (T47), 94
Gazelle Roll-Up aka Sea Horse (T48), 95-96
Half Bent Star (T50), 97
½ Angel (T37), 84-85
½ Angel Inversion aka Angel 3 (T38), 85
½ Angel on the Ropes (T82), 130-131
Hip Hang aka Single Knee Lay Back aka Amazon aka Gazelle (T47), 94
Inverted Angel aka Zoe Trick (T77), 124
Iron Cross aka Flag on the Ropes (T80), 128
Knee Hang Beat aka Rock & Roll Up (T29), 73
L aka Pike (T09), 55
Leg-Up Side Lay back aka Star variation (T12), 58
L-Up aka Rock & Roll (T09), 55
Mermaid aka Twisting Lay Back aka Fish (T31), 75
Monkey Roll aka Forward Roll (T67), 115
Monkey Roll onto the Bar aka Double Knee Roll-Up aka Russian Roll-Up (T42), 90
Moscow Angel (T83), 132
One Arm Stand aka Amazon (T43), 91
One Legged Birds Nest aka ¼ Angel (T16), 62
One Leg Monkey Roll aka One Leg Russian Roll aka Single Knee Roll Up (T30), 74

One Leg Russian Roll aka Single Knee Roll Up aka One Leg Monkey Roll (T30), 74
Open Angel (T39), 86-87
Pike aka L ((T09), 55
Proper Body Position 45-46
Pullover 48
Pullover from standing on the ground (T24), 71
¼ Angel aka One Legged Birds Nest (T16), 62
¼ Angel on the Ropes (T70), 118
Rainbow Split aka Straddle (T23), 70
Rainbow Split on the Ropes (T71), 119
Rock & Roll aka L-Up, (T09), 55
Rock & Roll Up aka Knee Hang Beat (T29), 73
Roll Over aka Foot Flag (T32), 76
Roll-Through (T33), 77-79
Rope Splits aka Snowflake (T79), 126-127
Russian Roll-Up aka Monkey Roll onto the Bar aka Double Knee Roll-Up (T42), 90
Sea Horse aka Gazelle Roll-Up (T48), 95-96
Scissor Roll (T58), 106
Scissor Roll Around (G59), 107
Scissor Sit aka Cuddle (T57), 105
Shoulder Wrap (T81), 129
Side Lay Back (T11), 57
Single Knee Hang (T86), 135
Single Knee Lay Back aka Hip Hang aka aka Amazon aka Gazelle (T47), 94
Single Knee Roll Up aka One Leg Russian Roll aka One Leg Monkey Roll (T30), 74
Single Point Trapeze 176-179
Sitting Lay Back on the Ropes (T76), 123
Sitting Poses (T46), 93
Skin the Cat aka Backwards Dismount (T87), 136
Snowflake aka Rope Splits (T79), 126-127
Splits (T13), 59-60
Split on the Ropes (T74), 121
Squat Routine (T20), 66
Squat to Air Split (T22), 69
Standing Lay Back (T17), 62
Standing Lay Back Split (T78), 125
Standing Side Lay Back (T66), 114
Standing Swing (T21), 67-68

Standing Up Gracefully (T14), 61
Standing X (T65), 113
Star (T49), 97
Star variation aka Leg-Up Side Lay Back (T12), 58
Straddle aka Rainbow Split (T23), 70
Straight Up & Down (T72), 120
Style, 79
Swing while sitting (T10), 56
Twisting Lay Back aka Mermaid aka Fish (T31), 75
Wrapped Moscow angel (T84), 133
Zoe Trick aka Inverted Angel (T77), 124

Warm Ups and Cool Downs
Chi Kung, 20-23
- Brain Balancing, 23
- Spinal Rock aka Tuck, 21
- Tuck aka Spinal Rock, 21
- Waist, 22
- Warming Up the Spine, 20

Sample Stretches, 24-39
- Back Bend, 38
- Child's Pose, 37
- Cobra, 36
- Downward Dog, 30
- Foot and Ankle, 26
- Forward Bend aka Pike, 28
- Hips and Legs, 27
- Neck, 31
- Partner Straddle Stretch, 29
- Pike aka Forward Bend, 28
- Shoulder Stretches, 32-35
  - Rotator Cuff, 33-34
  - Wall Shoulder Stretch, 35
- Standing Back Bend, 39Lay Back
- Wrist and Forearms, 24-25

The Aerial Circus Training and Safety Manual

A GUIDE FOR TEACHERS AND STUDENTS

BY CARRIE HELLER, M.S.W.
Photos by Richard Lubrant
Foreword by Hovey Burgess

The cost of the book is $49.95 plus $5.00 per book shipping and handling

If you are ordering more than 4 books the quantity discounts will be as follows:

5-9 books	5% off books, shipping + handling charges
10-25 books	10% off books, shipping + handling charges
26-59 books	15% off books, shipping + handling charges
50 books or more	20% off books, shipping + handling charges

ORDER FORM

1. # of books ordered x Price per book = Total cost of book   = _____

2. # of books ordered x $5 per shipping + handling   = _____

Your Quantity discount if 5 or more books ordered (5, 10, 15 or 20%) = _____

Total cost of books x discount = _____ = Total price of books + shipping

Please mail your check with this form to:

Circus Arts Institute
206 Rogers St. NE, Suite 214
Atlanta, GA 30317
phone: (404)549-3000   email: carrie@circusartsinstitute.com

Ship To:

Name_____

Address_____

City_____ State_____ Zip_____

e-mail_____ Phone_____

Notes:

Notes:

Notes:

Notes: